CAMBRIDGE
GED
PROGRAM

NEW REVISED

CAMBRIDGE GED PROGRAM

EXERCISE BOOK FOR **Writing Skills Part I**

CAMBRIDGE ADULT EDUCATION
A Division of Simon & Schuster
Upper Saddle River, New Jersey

NEW REVISED CAMBRIDGE GED PROGRAM

WRITERS
Beverly Ann Chin
Gloria Levine
Karen Wunderman
Stella Sands
Michael Ross
Alan Hines
Donald Gerstein

CONSULTANTS/REVIEWERS
Marjorie Jacobs
Cecily Bodnar
Diane Hardison
Dr. Margaret Tinzmann
Nora Chomitz
Bert C. Honigman
Sylvester Pues

COVER
Art Director: Josée Ungaretta
Cover Design: Marta Wolchuk, Design Five, NYC
Cover Illustration: Min Jae Hong

Printed in the United States of America

3 4 5 6 7 8 9 10   01 00 99

ISBN 0-835-94746-7

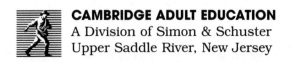

CAMBRIDGE ADULT EDUCATION
A Division of Simon & Schuster
Upper Saddle River, New Jersey

Contents

INTRODUCTION

This *Exercise Book for the Writing Skills Test, Part One* can help you prepare for the Part 1 of the GED's Writing Skills Test. You can use it along with either the *New Revised Cambridge GED Program: Comprehensive Book* or the *New Revised Cambridge GED Program: Writing Skills.*

The Three Sections of this Book

This book has three sections: Exercise, Practice, and Simulation. All three sections share a common purpose—to provide you with practice at the writing skills that you need when you take the GED. The paragraphs that follow explain what each section of this book is and tell you how to use it to your best advantage.

The Exercise Section

What Is the Exercise Section? The Exercise Section allows you to practice one writing skill at a time. It is made up of activities grouped according to the chapters, skills, and lessons in the Unit I instruction section of both the *New Revised Cambridge GED Program: Comprehensive Book* and the *New Revised GED Program: Writing Skills.* There is a group of exercises for each lesson in the grammar and editing unit of either book. The exercises concentrate on one aspect of grammar and editing at a time. The questions follow various formats, but all the Chapter 4 questions are multiple choice, as on the actual GED.

How to Use The Exercise Section. After you complete a lesson in either of the Cambridge Programs, you can get practice by using the corresponding exercise in this book. This allows you to practice with skills you have just studied in order to reinforce them. If you'd rather, however, you can wait until after you've studied all the lessons in a skill or chapter, and then complete the related exercises. It would probably be best for you to complete the exercises in this book before you work on the corresponding Practice Items in the textbooks.

The Practice Tests

What Are the Practice Tests? This book has two practice tests that are structured like Part 1 of the actual Writing Skills Test of the GED. The writing and editing skills you need to use vary from item to item, just as on the real test. The first test, the Half-length Practice Test, is made up of 28 items—about half as many as make up the actual GED. The second practice test has 55 items, the same length as the real test. Both tests give you an opportunity to practice taking a test similar to the GED.

How to Use the Practice Tests. You should take the Practice Tests after you have completed Unit I in either *Cambridge GED Program* and the exercises in this book. You may want to take the Practice Tests in this book after you complete the Practice section in either textbook. The Half-length Practice Test should take 38 minutes. The Full-length Practice Test should take 75 minutes, the same amount of time allowed on Part 1 of the actual Writing Skills Test.

The Simulated Test

What Is the Simulated Test? The Simulated Test is as much like the actual GED test as possible. It has two parts and the same number of questions as the real test. As on the Practice Tests, the type of writing skill you need to apply varies from item to item. Taking the Simulated Test will help you determine how ready you are to take the real GED test.

How to Use the Simulated Test. You can take the Simulated Test before or after you've taken the Simulated Writing Skills Test in either of the Cambridge GED Programs. Take the Simulated Test under the same conditions as you will have when you take the real Writing Skills Test—work without interruption and do not talk to anyone or consult any other materials. You should complete Part I of the Simulated Test in 75 minutes, the same amount of time you will have on the actual GED. Allow yourself 45 minutes for Part II.

Scoring Your Work and Using Your Scores

You will find the Answers and Explanations at the back of the book to be a very useful study tool. When you complete a section in this book, compare your answers to the correct answers given. Whether you answer an item correctly or not, you should read through the explanation. Doing this will reinforce your writing and editing skills and develop your test taking skills. After you check you answers to the items on one of the three tests, you can complete the appropriate Performance Analysis Chart. The charts can help you determine which writing and editing skills you are strongest in, and direct you to parts of the Cambridge Programs where you can review areas in which you need additional work.

CHAPTER 1
Usage

Skill 1

Subject-Verb Agreement

Lesson 1   The Basics of Subject-Verb Agreement

DIRECTIONS: Edit the sentences to correct all errors in subject-verb agreement. Not all the sentences have errors.

1. Everybody help to clean up the house on Saturday mornings.
2. The committee members was discussing the issue before the vote.
3. Most concerts this season were delightful.
4. Many children enjoys building sand castles at the beach.
5. Few meteors was sighted during the skywatch.
6. The personnel director post the list of job openings once a month.
7. Mechanical refrigeration systems were first patented in 1834.
8. No one have failed to notice the new maple trees in the park.
9. The jury are prepared to announce its verdict.
10. Many houses benefits from additional insulation.

Answers are on page 75.

Lesson 2   Interrupting Phrases

DIRECTIONS: Edit the following sentences to correct all the errors in subject-verb agreement. Not all the sentences have errors.

1. The shortest distance between two points are a straight line.
2. Several proposals for a mass transit system includes the construction of a monorail.
3. The asparagus plant, along with several varieties of beans, grow easily in this soil.
4. One of the first number systems in recorded history was the Babylonian.
5. Accuracy in design and production have earned a good reputation for that tool company.
6. Tea, as well as coffee and many soft drinks, contain caffeine.
7. Physics, as well as chemistry, are a required course for third-year students.
8. The location of a house are one factor affecting the selling price.
9. Yorkshire terriers, as well as poodles, are popular dogs in France.
10. One of Robert Frost's most famous poems are "Birches."

Answers are on page 75.

Lesson 3 Inverted Sentence Structure

DIRECTIONS: Edit the following sentences to correct all the errors in subject-verb agreement. Not all the sentences have errors.

1. At the concert was Jane and her brothers.
2. Was the results of the diving competition already announced?
3. Because of the heavy traffic, many employees were late for work.
4. For many reasons, Jerry enjoys his new job.
5. Are the new communications system more efficient than the old one?
6. On the lake was a swan and several geese.
7. Around the playground run a high fence.
8. On each side of the road was signs advertising restaurants.
9. Was the hurricane as dangerous as last year's storm?
10. Are the quality of those shirts related to the price?

Answers are on pages 75–76.

Lesson 4 *Here* and *There*

DIRECTIONS: Edit the following sentences to correct all the errors in subject-verb agreement. Not all the sentences have errors.

1. Here is the most recent issues of that magazine.
2. Here was the site of the Boston Tea Party.
3. There was approximately one million inhabitants of the city of Rome in ancient times.
4. Here is the house where Mark Twain lived in Hartford, Connecticut.
5. There is six states in the New England region.
6. Here are the money I owe you for lunch last week.
7. There is about 40 million Americans affected by diabetes and its related diseases.
8. Here is the new radio and earphones you ordered.
9. There is 1500 languages and dialects spoken in India.
10. There is three television debates scheduled between the candidates.

Answers are on page 76.

Lesson 5 Compound Subjects

DIRECTIONS: Edit the following sentences to correct all the errors in subject-verb agreement. Not all the sentences have errors.

1. Both a keyboard and a monitor is basic parts of a computer system.
2. Either Irma or her sister are planning to compete in the race.
3. Either the captain or the flight attendants make the announcement.
4. Neither the pay nor the working conditions was satisfactory in that office.
5. Either Rick or Phil have repaired the chairs.
6. Peter and his cousins have enjoyed their annual camping trips.
7. Neither the governor nor the lieutenant governor have signed this bill into law.
8. Sue and her sister have still not been given a raise.
9. Not only the town's mayor but also the chief of police are African American.
10. Either the doctor or the nurse give the injections.

Answers are on page 76.

Verb Tense

Lesson 1   Verb Forms

DIRECTIONS: Complete the following sentences by adding the verb in the tense indicated in parentheses.

1. Drunk drivers _____ many fatal accidents each year on the nation's highways. (cause, present tense)

2. In ancient times, many people _____ that omens predicted the future. (think, past tense)

3. Last spring, the tulips _____ very well in this soil. (grow, past tense)

4. Hank may have problems if he _____ to accept that job. (choose, present tense)

5. The average building on this block _____ eight apartments. (contain, present tense)

DIRECTIONS: Complete the following sentences by adding the past participle of the verb given in parentheses.

6. Have you _____ the car all the way to Indianapolis? (drive)

7. Martha has _____ down for quite a while. (lie)

8. The geese always take flight several minutes after the sun has _____ . (rise)

9. Chuck admits that he has _____ about the job opening since he told Randy about it. (know)

10. Are they aware of what they have _____ ? (do)

Answers are on page 76.

Lesson 2   Word Clues to Tense in Sentences

DIRECTIONS: Edit the following sentences to correct all the errors in verb tense. Not all the sentences have errors.

1. The first modern income tax is assessed in England around 1800.

2. Next Saturday, the Rangers have played the Bruins.

3. Do you think that Robert has received his degree next year?

4. The Civil War takes place between 1861 and 1865.

5. Today, many people took mass transportation to get to work.

6. Admission to the museum is free on Sundays.

7. Last week, Helen will receive a perfect score on her geography test.

8. The catalytic converter reduces pollution from automobiles for the last five years.

9. At the moment, I am not able to tell you the exact answer.

10. John has met us later after the movie.

Answers are on page 77.

Lesson 3   Word Clues to Tense in Context

DIRECTIONS: The following paragraphs contain a mixture of the present and past tense. Rewrite the paragraphs in the appropriate tense. Not all the sentences will have to be changed.

1. An earthquake is a violent movement of the Earth's surface. Earthquakes sometimes began with slight tremors and then increased in the intensity of the shock. The most common cause of earthquakes is a sudden stress along a fault line in the Earth's crust. This stress led to vibrations that pass through the Earth. A scale called the Richter scale measures the amount of energy released by a quake.

2. When we visit New York last year at Christmas, the city was magical. Many department stores have lovely window displays, and the streets are full of holiday shoppers. We visited Central Park, which glistened in the snow, and we attend several concerts. I especially enjoy seeing the great tree at Rockefeller Center. Since our whole family is together for the first time in many months, the trip was a special treat.

Answers are on page 77.

Lesson 4   Using Tenses Consistently

DIRECTIONS: Edit the following sentences for correct sequence of tenses. Choose the correct verb from the pair given in parentheses.

1. Light bulbs were on sale yesterday, and Mrs. Polk (buys, bought) a dozen.
2. When the gates open, cars (were, will be) able to proceed.
3. Forecasters predict that snow (fell, will fall) later this week in the mountains.
4. When the runners finally came into the stretch, we (saw, see) that Marla was leading.
5. Sam thinks that the voters (send, will send) the mayor a message next November.
6. That deli is new, and the sandwiches (will be, are) some of the best I have ever eaten.
7. As the threats to world peace multiply, the price of gold generally (rose, rises).
8. Cats are popular pets, and they soon (outnumber, will outnumber) dogs in American households.
9. As clouds covered the sun, the temperature (falls, fell).
10. Few tall buildings are to be seen in that city, because earthquakes frequently (occur, occurred) there.

Answers are on page 77.

Skill 3 — Pronoun Reference

Skill 3

Lesson 1   Pronouns: Agreement with Antecedent

DIRECTIONS: Edit the following sentences to correct all the errors in pronoun-antecedent agreement. Not all the sentences have errors.

1. Some people like to record his thoughts every day in a diary.
2. A governor or a mayor must be attentive to the needs of their constituents.
3. The United States and Canada sent its leaders to the economic conference.
4. Orchestra members bring their instruments with them to the concert.
5. Marv and Jim were proud of his team's new record.
6. The commuters boarded his bus at 7:30 a.m.
7. The neighbors kindly invited us to our party.
8. Slipping on the ice, Mrs. Pennington fell and bruised its knee.
9. To succeed, a newspaper or a magazine must appeal to their readers.
10. The president told his audience that he would not seek re-election.

Answers are on pages 77–78.

Lesson 2   Avoiding Pronoun Shifts

DIRECTIONS: Edit the following sentences to correct all errors in pronoun shift. Not all the sentences have errors.

1. When you interview for a job, we should remember to be courteous.
2. You should not eat so much cheese if we are trying to lose weight.
3. Ambitious people will always aim for perfection in everything you do.
4. When you buy an appliance, they should always save your receipt.
5. If you have any side-effects from that medicine, see your doctor immediately.
6. On the first day of your new job, try to learn all we can about your responsibilities.
7. If we have any vacation time this summer, they will visit our relatives in Nebraska.
8. When you see that movie, you will be on the edge of their seat!
9. Exercise can relieve one's mental stress as well as improve their physical condition.
10. Before you board the plane, you will have to check your baggage at the counter.

Answers are on page 78.

Lesson 3   Relative Pronouns

DIRECTIONS: Edit the following sentences to correct all the errors in relative pronoun usage. Not all the sentences have errors.

1. In English class, the writer which I enjoyed most was Edgar Allan Poe.
2. The Canadian goose is a bird what migrates to our area in the winter.
3. The painter whom I admire most is Georgia O'Keefe.

4. Visitors to Washington which see the Lincoln Memorial seldom fail to be impressed.

5. The flowers whom I planted in the early spring have all bloomed.

6. The article what I read predicted a sharp increase in car sales.

7. Shoppers whom present this coupon are eligible for a discount.

8. St. Paul, which is the capital of Minnesota, is on the banks of the Mississippi River.

9. Ponce de Leon, who governed Puerto Rico in the early sixteenth century, was also the discoverer of Florida.

10. The cardinal, who is a member of the finch family, has a crest and a red bill.

Answers are on page 78.

Lesson 4   Avoiding Vague Pronoun References

DIRECTIONS: Edit the following sentences to correct all errors in vague pronoun reference. You might have to rewrite or add word(s) to the sentences. Not all sentences have errors.

1. Clara is on vacation, which is why she is not in the office this week.

2. Jenna wants to be a salesperson because they earn good commissions.

3. The governor has spoken in favor of that proposal, whom the majority of the state's voters support.

4. In a newspaper I read, they wrote an interesting article about Alaska.

5. Not paying subway fare, which is high, is against the law.

6. This exhibit is very popular, which is why the lines to get into the museum are so long.

7. John wants to study for a career in medicine because they are dedicated to helping people.

8. Although the fire broke out at 10:00 p.m., they did not reach the house until fifteen minutes later.

9. The meteorologists predicted high winds on the lake, which is why the fishing expedition was canceled.

10. John and his sister want to study engineering because they will be in demand in the coming decades.

Answers are on pages 78–79.

Lesson 5   Avoiding Ambiguous Pronoun References

DIRECTIONS: Edit the following items to correct all errors in ambiguous pronoun reference.

1. Because of his new proposal, the mayor and the treasurer were criticized in today's editorial.

2. The director told the actor that he needed a new approach.

3. One of my nephews told my father that he would get a raise.

4. The most famous novel of Cervantes is Don Quixote. He was a romantic adventurer.

5. The librarian reminded Paul that he had already read that book.

6. The directors told the shareholders that they could not expect the company to make a profit this year.

7. One of Mark Twain's novels is about life on the Mississippi. It is very colorful.

8. Our cousins told the neighbors that their taxes were too high.

9. This magazine carries many articles about exotic animals. They are fascinating.

10. Our friends told the bus drivers that they were going to be late.

Answers are on page 79.

CHAPTER 2
Sentence Structure

Skill 1 — Complete Sentences

Lesson 1   Eliminating Sentence Fragments

DIRECTIONS: Edit the following items to correct all sentence-fragment errors. Not all the items have errors.

1. The Mississippi River the longest river in North America.
2. Reached a verdict after three hours.
3. The reward for a hard day's work.
4. Although several inches of snow fell during the night.
5. Found the ten-mile race exhausting.
6. Many American carpet manufacturers are located in Georgia.
7. The term "canoe" referring to several types of thin, long boats.
8. Canada the largest country in the Western Hemisphere.
9. The cashew tree is related to poison ivy.
10. Early people creating art on the walls of caves.

Answers are on pages 79–80.

Lesson 2   Eliminating Run-on Sentences

DIRECTIONS: Edit the following items to correct all run-on sentences. Not all the items have errors.

1. The Rose Bowl is one of the country's largest stadiums, it is located in California.
2. The chipmunk is a kind of squirrel there are more than 300 kinds of squirrels.
3. Mississippi's first newspaper was published in 1799, today 25 daily newspapers are published in that state.
4. Spiders do not have teeth, they eat only liquids.
5. The stagecoach was used to transport passengers and mail, sometimes it also carried freight.
6. Shirley Chisholm was the first black woman to serve in the U.S. Congress, she was elected in 1968.
7. The sponge was once considered a plant it is actually an animal.
8. Philadelphia is the largest city in Pennsylvania, it is the fourth largest city in the country.

9. The human heart is a muscle. It pumps blood throughout the body.

10. The sport of paddle tennis was invented in 1898 city championships were first held in New York City in 1922.

Answers are on page 80.

Lesson 3   Other Ways of Eliminating Run-on Sentences

DIRECTIONS: Edit the following items to correct all run-on sentences. Not all the items have errors.

1. The zoo in Philadelphia opened in 1874, it is the oldest zoo in the country.

2. Butter has been used throughout history for many unusual purposes for example ancient Romans used it as a skin cream.

3. The development of a pearl within an oyster is a slow process, it may take three years for an oyster to produce a valuable pearl.

4. Brazil is the largest country in South America and has more farmland than all Europe.

5. Red-winged blackbirds live in marshes they build their nests in the rushes.

6. Plants are the source of all our food the study of plants is important.

7. The construction was not completed on schedule the client withheld payment.

8. Herbs are widely used in cooking, many herbs are native to the Mediterranean countries.

9. Musk turtles eat anything, they prefer to eat animal food.

10. The southern states cover only about one-seventh of the country nearly one-quarter of the American people live in the region.

Answers are on page 80.

Coordination and Subordination

Lesson 1   Coordination

DIRECTIONS: Edit the following sentences to correct all errors in sentence coordination. Some sentences should not be combined. Not all the sentences have errors.

1. The influence of refrigerated railroad cars was great; however, fresh foods could travel vast distances without spoiling.

2. The first record of the potato, which is native to South America, was made in 1533; however, it may have been taken to Europe by 1550.

3. Many people registered to vote, so the upcoming election is an important one.

4. Some kinds of pelicans can fly for hours, so the pelican is one of the largest birds with webbed feet.

5. Alabama's first television station was established in 1949; on the other hand, the state's first radio station was founded 27 years earlier.

6. Fresh-water aquariums are inexpensive and easily maintained; nevertheless, many people enjoy owning them.

7. Ragweed grows quickly and is not easily noticed; otherwise, efforts to eliminate it have failed.

8. Quilting parties were common in the American colonies, but quilting is still a popular hobby.

9. The Grand Canyon was formed by glaciers and rushing water, and hundreds of tourists admire the sight each year.

10. The Industrial Revolution began in Britain, Britain has produced many important inventions.

Answers are on pages 80–81.

Lesson 2   Subordination

DIRECTIONS: Edit the following sentences to correct all subordination errors. Not all the sentences have errors.

1. Because democracy requires the participation of all citizens, then it is important to vote.

2. Until before the advent of films with sound, a movie actor's voice was of no importance.

3. Although letters are usually appreciated they are rarely written.

4. While some large lakes are called seas, although a lake is usually a fairly small body of water surrounded by land.

5. Even though the library is open, you can listen to records or tapes.

6. Because the petals of columbine hold large amounts of nectar, hummingbirds and bees are attracted to this flower.

7. Unless it is cooked eggplant is not pleasant to eat.

8. As long as the clothing industry is an international business, so people in many countries will dress similarly.

9. As soon as the band started to play, we knew the parade had begun.

10. Whenever he was invited to speak, thus Wilson gladly gave his opinion.

Answers are on page 81.

Lesson 3   Combining Sentences

DIRECTIONS: Edit the following pairs of sentences to make them less repetitious.

1. Ralph lent Maureen a fishing rod. Ralph lent Maureen a reel.

2. The letter concerned Ruth's tax return. The telephone call concerned Ruth's tax return.

3. He noticed the full moon. He knew it was time to go to sleep.

4. Mr. Baker sold eighteen of the sandwiches. Mr. Baker had hoped to sell them all.

5. One large country is Australia. One sparsely populated country is Australia.

6. The new restaurant is popular. The new restaurant does not accept reservations.

7. My neighbor rides the bus to work each day. Alex rides the bus to work each day.

8. The history of the flute is interesting. The history of the flute is not commonly known.

9. Ruby bought the novel as soon as it was published. Ruby has not read it yet.

10. I saw Dennis at the grocery store. I saw Miss Westin at the pharmacy.

Answers are on page 81.

Lesson 1   Clarity of Thought

DIRECTIONS: Edit the following sentences to correct all errors in clarity. Not all the sentences have errors.

1. The final result surprised the governor in the end.

2. Alice Johnson interviewed the athlete before she had lunch.

3. The parties involved, all being duly employed by the company, have brought their request for an increase in wages before their manager.

4. The proprietor of the establishment made an inquiry in a discreet fashion for the customers to give payment.

5. Our two choices were either to put off and postpone the meeting or to go ahead and proceed as planned.

6. The newspaper is printed with a greasy ink; it is inexpensive.

7. Radiance borne through the air from the sun shone through the window.

8. Jogger #10 ran next to #3 until she suddenly raced ahead.

9. The crowd totaled 85 people in number and was one of patience in waiting.

10. The singer met the soloist after he performed.

Answers are on pages 81–82.

Lesson 2   Proper Modification

DIRECTIONS: Edit the following sentences to correct all modification errors. You may need to add one or more words. Not all the sentences have errors.

1. Many people dislike vegetables such as broccoli and cauliflower when they are young.

2. Reaching the corner, the traffic light changed to red.

3. Exhausted by the long tour, we were glad to return to our hotel.

4. Albert gazed at the painting forgetting his appointment.

5. When I spoke with you earlier, I asked you promptly to pay the bill.

6. Rita discovered her watch had stopped waiting for the train.

7. Blooming in the spring, Holland is covered with acres of tulips.

8. Lois ran silently up the stairs and opened the tiny package.

9. Mr. Alcorn bought three boxes of detergent at the supermarket on sale.

10. I brought a kitten home with a black spot on its nose.

Answers are on page 82.

DIRECTIONS: Edit these sentences to correct all errors in parallel structure. Not all the sentences have errors.

1. The concept of democracy was bold, innovative, and involved some risk.

2. Neither loss of appetite nor to be dizzy is a side-effect of her medication.

3. To bridge, budding, and clefting are three types of grafting familiar to most gardeners.

4. Major milestones in child development include learning to see, walk, and speech.

5. Training horses, flying, and to write were Beryl Markham's primary accomplishments.

6. Physicians strive to detect, cure, and the prevention of disease.

7. The safety of the passengers, the reliability of the equipment, and whether the system was efficient were the controller's greatest concerns.

8. Architecture, dance, photography, and travel were among Eddie's interests.

9. Kim said the finest contributions of the twentieth century were the paper napkin, the ball point pen, and to make a disposable razor.

10. Firefighters need to possess physical strength, be able to work under pressure, and thinking quickly.

Answers are on page 82.

CHAPTER 3
Mechanics

Capitalization

Lesson 1   Proper Nouns and Proper Adjectives

DIRECTIONS: Edit the following sentences to correct all capitalization errors. There may be more than one error in each sentence. Not all sentences have errors.

1. New orleans is the largest city in the state of louisiana.

2. My grandmother has always been especially fond of chinese food.

3. Much portuguese fish is exported to other European countries.

4. One of the most famous zoos in the world is located in san diego, California.

5. Languages commonly spoken in Switzerland include german, french, English, and Italian.

6. The trees along Main Street are maintained by the village improvement society.

7. Lake Ontario is somewhat smaller than Lake Erie.

8. On our trip to Washington, we visited the Senate and the house of representatives.

9. Istanbul, Ankara, and Izmir are three of the principal cities in Turkey.

10. We left the Northeast and drove South to Miami, Florida.

Answers are on pages 82–83.

Lesson 2   Titles of People and Addresses

DIRECTIONS: Edit the following sentences to correct all capitalization errors. Not all the sentences have errors.

1. Each state is entitled to two Senators and to a different number of Representatives, according to its population.

2. I saw uncle Henry at the graduation ceremony.

3. Dr. Johnson has office hours every afternoon between 2:00 and 5:00.

4. We told Irene to speak to our Mother about plans for the picnic.

5. The White House is located at 1600 Pennsylvania avenue in Washington, D.C.

6. Rajiv lives three blocks south of the highway, on Elm Street.

7. Our aunt's relatives asked reverend Foster to perform the service.

8. Have you seen the new construction taking place on Williams Avenue?

9. I told Susan to ask ms. Santos, the Director of Public Welfare, about that telephone call.

10. This matter will have to be decided by mayor Weston.

Answers are on page 83.

Lesson 3   Time, Dates, Seasons, Special Events, and Historical Eras

DIRECTIONS: Edit the following sentences to correct all capitalization errors. Not all the sentences have errors.

1. Heavy snowfalls in Winter are not unusual in Maine.

2. The last day of the year is december 31.

3. Nero was one of the cruelest rulers of the roman empire.

4. World War II began in Europe in the year 1939.

5. Michelangelo and Leonardo Da Vinci were two of the greatest artists of the renaissance.

6. The test begins at 9 a.m.

7. Thanksgiving Day occurs on the fourth thursday of November.

8. The Vietnam war took place during the 1960s and 1970s.

9. In that part of Finland, sunset is seldom before 11 P.M. during the summer months.

10. New Year's day is an occasion for visits and presents in Japan.

Answers are on page 83.

Skill
2

Lesson 1   Commas in a Series

DIRECTIONS: Edit the following sentences to correct all punctuation errors. Not all the sentences have errors.

1. The talented, lively, and intelligent, actress gave a marvelous television interview.

2. The major factors in the value of a house are size, location, and condition.

3. Tall, slender, graceful, trees surround the clearing.

4. This firm can design hotel rooms and lobbies, private residences, and offices.

5. Participation in sports can increase the motivation, teamwork, and, leadership abilities of many students.

6. Lisa bent down to examine a small dark red shell on the beach.

7. We are interested in buying a car that has cruise control, and power windows.

8. The trembling frightened bird sat on the window ledge.

9. Three popular breeds of cat are the Siamese, the Burmese, and the Persian.

10. When I am in New York, I will visit the Metropolitan Museum, and the Bronx Zoo, and the Empire State Building, and the World Trade Center.

Answers are on pages 83–84.

Lesson 2   Commas in Compound Sentences

DIRECTIONS: Edit the following sentences to correct all punctuation errors. Not all the sentences have errors.

1. Our office recently purchased a new computer and now, many jobs can be finished more quickly.

2. Land prices in this town are rising quickly for the area is extremely attractive to out-of-state residents.

3. The court will have to rule on Ms. Tarn's petition or she will file an appeal.

4. Municipal zoos provide pleasure to many people but the care of the animals has often been questioned.

5. You can buy the tools at the local hardware store, or make a special trip into Madison to get them.

6. Many excavations in China are still in the planning stage and archaeologists have hopes of discovering new treasures.

7. The plane landed safely and the passengers cheered.

8. Tom signed up for the chemistry course in college because he wanted to satisfy the pre-med requirements.

9. The price of gasoline will have to come down or Americans will take fewer vacation trips this summer.

10. The mayor flatly opposes the new housing project, but many people think he will change his mind.

Answers are on page 84.

Lesson 3   Commas after Introductory Elements

DIRECTIONS: Edit the following sentences to correct all punctuation errors. Not all the sentences have errors.

1. Honored guests I would like to say a few words about the achievements of our principal speaker.
2. Controlling the waterway between Europe and Asia, Istanbul has been a strategic city throughout the centuries.
3. Hank I would like you to run for team captain.
4. When the heat was shut off in that building the pipes froze in the sub-zero weather and burst.
5. Yes the train will arrive 45 minutes late.
6. However we will be able to spend at least one day hiking this weekend.
7. Uncle Henry I'd like to introduce my friend Tim.
8. Handling hundreds of flights each day, the airport in Atlanta is one of the busiest in the world.
9. Moreover we did not realize that we should have checked the route carefully before setting out.
10. No he decided not to take that job.

Answers are on page 84.

Lesson 4   Commas with Sentence Interrupters

DIRECTIONS: Edit the following sentences to correct all punctuation errors. Not all the sentences have errors.

1. Susan Ramos our class president will address the assembly.
2. The musical, West Side Story, enjoyed a long run on Broadway.
3. The roof in my opinion needs patching in several places.
4. The Congo, one of the longest rivers in Africa, winds through several countries.
5. The capital of Oregon I believe is Salem.
6. You will I hope ask for a raise within the next month.
7. These models on the other hand have automatic transmission.
8. Our cousin Felipe is starting a new business.
9. The window nevertheless was open.
10. Football, in my opinion, is a more exciting sport than baseball.

Answers are on pages 84–85.

DIRECTIONS: Edit the following sentences to correct all punctuation errors. Not all the sentences have errors.

1. World War II ended in Europe in May of 1945, but, peace did not come in the Far East until August of that year.

2. Sue will spend the weekend studying, and her parents will go fishing.

3. Mr. Rescigno will visit Boston, Providence, and, Hartford.

4. Sandy bought, crackers, cheese, and, a head of lettuce at the store.

5. The fashion industry is centered in New York, and, the entertainment industry is based in Hollywood.

6. A short run, and a relaxing swim were what we needed that day.

7. One of the most famous paintings in the world, is called the Mona Lisa.

8. Mark Twain's novels and stories often contain clever, ironic, humor.

9. The three dogs ran, and played in the park.

10. The architect offered a creative, attractive solution to all the design problems.

Answers are on page 85.

Lesson 1   Basic Spelling Rules

DIRECTIONS: Edit the following sentences to correct all errors in spelling. No sentence has more than one error. Not all the sentences have errors.

1. At lunchtime, only one of the benchs in the park was empty.

2. Mysterys are Larry's favorite type of bedtime reading.

3. Even people who dislike most types of fishes will eat tuna salad sandwiches.

4. The hosts provided the knifes and forks for the pot luck supper.

5. After ploting out their route, the Jacksons left for vacation.

6. As a finishing touch, Julie doted the i on her sign, "Julie's Bakery—Open for Business."

7. Learning CPR can save lifes.

8. Last year, we finished wrapping the last of the Christmas presents after midnight.

9. The extra set of keyes is hanging up near the kitchen sink.

10. Jackets made from the hides of sheeps are popular in Colorado.

Answers are on page 85.

Lesson 2   Possessives

DIRECTIONS: Edit the following sentences to correct all errors in the spelling of possessive nouns and pronouns. Not all of the sentences have errors.

1. You buy your ticket and we will buy our's.

2. How much did you're new bicycle cost, Jim?

3. The doctors office was closed.

4. Susan B. Anthony was an important figure in the struggle for womens rights.

5. The states' governors gathered in Phoenix.

6. Did you ask mother which of these books were her's?

7. My cat likes to sleep on it's back.

8. The director's chair was placed to the left of the camera.

9. We asked Martha to put away the childrens' toys.

10. The orchestra's concerts were well reviewed.

Answers are on pages 85–86.

Lesson 3   Contractions

DIRECTIONS: Edit the following sentences to correct all errors in the spelling of contractions. Not all the sentences have errors.

1. Its true that Thomas Jefferson and John Adams both died on the same day, July 4, 1826.
2. I'd like to borrow you're copy of that novel.
3. Is'nt Peru located in South America?
4. Mark thinks he'd like to change jobs.
5. Im very grateful for your recommendation.
6. We're sorry that we did'nt see that play.
7. Tell Mr. Darby that we've already made the delivery.
8. We found out that the Richardsons intend to sell they're business.
9. The vegetables aren't overcooked, are they?
10. Lets all meet at the bus station at five o'clock.

Answers are on page 86.

Lesson 4   Homonyms

DIRECTIONS: Edit the following sentences to correct all homonym errors. Not all the sentences have errors. Some sentences may have more than one error.

1. Mustard compliments many different foods.
2. We told the instructor that our assignments were all ready completed.
3. I herd that Richard had a very successful interview.
4. When the flight was called, the passengers boarded the plain.
5. Integrity in government is an important principle.
6. A major issue now is the proper disposal of nuclear waists.
7. Usually their are nine innings in a baseball game.
8. Except for a few miner errors, the news article was accurate.
9. Does this car have reliable breaks?
10. An amendment will be required to altar the by-laws.

Answers are on page 86.

DIRECTIONS: One word is misspelled in each group of words. Circle the misspelled word and write the correct spelling of each word in the exercise.

1. accustomed
   aggressive
   almost
   attempt
   boundry

2. bulletin
   campaign
   cheif
   citizen
   column

3. communicate
   conceil
   conscience
   consistency
   courteous

4. criticizm
   cylinder
   disease
   decisive
   dilemma

5. dozen
   exaggerate
   February
   imaginary
   interupt

6. liesure
   magazine
   mathematics
   narrative
   negligence

7. opportunity
   pamphlet
   paralel
   perpendicular
   pleasant

8. posession
   predictable
   procedure
   quality
   realize

9. receipt
   rehearsal
   resource
   roommate
   seperate

10. sucessful
    technical
    tenant
    twelfth
    business

Answers are on page 86.

CHAPTER 4
Editing Paragraphs

Lesson 1   The Three Types of Questions on the GED Writing Skills Test

DIRECTIONS: The following sentences contain errors in sentence structure, usage, and mechanics. No sentence contains more than one error. Answer the questions that follow by circling the number of the one best answer for each question.

1. Sentence 1: **Despite the best efforts of each actor, last week's performances of the play was not successful.**

   What correction should be made to this sentence?

   (1) insert a comma after *efforts*
   (2) change *actor* to *actors*
   (3) remove the comma after *actor*
   (4) change *week's* to *weeks*
   (5) change *was* to *were*

2. Sentence 2: **When Anne worked in the Peace Corps she taught several foreign languages.**

   What correction should be made to this sentence?

   (1) change *Peace Corps* to *peace corps*
   (2) insert a comma after *Corps*
   (3) change the spelling of *foreign* to *foriegn*
   (4) change *languages* to *language*
   (5) no correction is necessary

3. Sentence 3: **My Uncle Max is prominent in our school because he is our principal.**

   What correction should be made to this sentence?

   (1) change *Uncle* to *uncle*
   (2) change the spelling of *prominent* to *prominant*
   (3) insert a comma after *school*
   (4) change *principal* to *principle*
   (5) no correction is necessary

4. Sentence 4: **There is, I believe, truth in his remark that is, people often do the right thing for the wrong reason.**

   What correction should be made to this sentence?

   (1) change the spelling of *believe* to *beleive*
   (2) remove the comma after *believe*
   (3) insert a semicolon after *remark*
   (4) insert a comma after *thing*
   (5) change the spelling of *reason* to *reasen*

5. Sentence 5: **Responsible journalists need to master many skills; they must be able to write accurately.**

What correction should be made to this sentence?

(1) insert *otherwise* after the semi-colon
(2) change the semi-colon to a comma
(3) remove the semi-colon after *skills*
(4) insert *for instance*, after the semi-colon
(5) change the spelling of *Responsible* to *Responsable*

6. Sentence 6: **A fresh plantain looks like a <u>banana but taste</u> bitter and tart.**

Which of the following is the best way to write the underlined portion of this sentence? If you think the original is the best way, choose option (1).

(1) banana but taste
(2) banana but tastes
(3) banana, but tastes
(4) banana. It tasted
(5) banana but tasted

7. Sentence 7: **Jean did not water the vegetable garden. She noticed the rain had begun to fall.**

If you rewrote sentence 7 beginning with

<u>Jean noticed the rain had begun to fall</u>,

the next word should be

(1) after
(2) but
(3) so
(4) because
(5) when

8. Sentence 8: **Just before the White House was burned by British soldiers, Dolly Madison leaves the building.**

What correction should be made to this sentence?

(1) insert a comma after *before*
(2) change *burned* to *burning*
(3) capitalize the word *soldiers*
(4) remove the comma after *soldiers*
(5) change *leaves* to *left*

9. Sentence 9: **This plant is able to survive extreme neglect; however, if <u>properly cared for it</u> produces charming flowers.**

Which of the following is the best way to write the underlined portion of this sentence? If you think the original is the best way, choose option (1).

(1) properly cared for it
(2) properly, cared for it
(3) properly, cared for, it
(4) properly cared for, it
(5) properly cared for it,

10. Sentence 10: **The giant panda is often mistaken for a bear. It is related to the raccoon.**

If you rewrote sentence 10 beginning with

<u>The giant panda is related to the raccoon;</u>

the next word should be

(1) however
(2) besides
(3) in addition
(4) for example
(5) consequently

Answers are on pages 86–87.

DIRECTIONS: The following paragraph contains errors in usage, sentence structure, and mechanics. No sentence contains more than one error. Use the 5-R method of editing to work through the first six items and to record your response at each step.

Step 1. *Read* Quickly read the paragraph for its meaning, writing style, verb tense, and pronoun usage.

Step 2. *Reflect* Read through the paragraph, underlining errors that you can recognize. Ask yourself: Is it correct? complete? clear?

Step 3. *Revise* Read the first item and its alternatives. Decide which alternative identifies and corrects the error.

Step 4. *Reread* Read the revised sentence with the selected correction. If you are satisfied with the answer, you are ready to go on to the next step. If you are not satisfied with the answer, go back to Step 3.

Step 5. *Record* Mark the number of the alternative that you have chosen. Then move on to the next item.

Your final answer should be written on the line for Step 5.

Items 1 to 10 are based on the following paragraph.

(1) One of the primary influences on regional cooking are geography. (2) Today, foods from all areas are accessible throughout the world; before this time, cooks had to make do with what they had. (3) Different climates fostered different types of plants and animals thus people of a region used the ingredients they found to invent their own distinctive dishes. (4) Because national borders are not always defined by geography, it is common for several types of regional cooking to exist in one country. (5) For example, any cook in Ecuador what uses traditional recipes belongs to one of two different regions. (6) The lowlands lie along the Pacific ocean. (7) Regional cooks of the lowlands have made great use of fish and seafood, such as lobster shrimp and black conch. (8) On the other hand, people of the highlands the steep hills surrounding the Andes Mountains, do not have access to fish. (9) They do, however, have potatoes, which are easily grown, stored, and to cook at high altitudes. (10) The potato is a major ingredient in ecuadorian highland cooking.

1. Sentence 1: **One of the primary influences on regional cooking are geography.**

   What correction should be made to this sentence?

   (1) insert a comma after *one*
   (2) change *influences* to *influence*
   (3) change the spelling of *influences* to *influenses*
   (4) change *are* to *is*
   (5) no correction is necessary

   Step 1.   Read: _____
   Step 2.   Reflect: _____
   Step 3.   Revise: _____
   Step 4.   Reread: _____
   Step 5.   Record: _____

2. Sentence 2: **Today, foods from all areas are accessible throughout the world; before this time, cooks had to make do with what they had.**

If you rewrote sentence 2 beginning with

Before foods from all areas became accessible throughout the world,

the next word should be

(1) however

(2) then

(3) cooks

(4) today

(5) so

Step 1.	Read:	_____
Step 2.	Reflect:	_____
Step 3.	Revise:	_____
Step 4.	Reread:	_____
Step 5.	Record:	_____

3. Sentence 3: **Different climates fostered different types of <u>plants and animals thus people</u> of a region used the ingredients they found to invent their own distinctive dishes.**

Which of the following is the best way to write the underlined portion of this sentence? If you think the original is the best way, choose option (1).

(1) plants and animals thus people

(2) plants and animals, thus people

(3) plants, and animals, thus people

(4) plants and animals; thus, people

(5) plants; and animals, thus people,

Step 1.	Read:	_____
Step 2.	Reflect:	_____
Step 3.	Revise:	_____
Step 4.	Reread:	_____
Step 5.	Record:	_____

4. Sentence 4: **Because national borders are not always defined by geography, it is common for several types of regional cooking to exist in one country.**

What correction should be made to this sentence?

(1) replace the comma after *geography* with a semicolon

(2) replace to *exist* with *have existed*

(3) change the spelling of *exist* to *exsist*

(4) insert a comma after *exist*

(5) no correction is necessary

Step 1.	Read:	_____
Step 2.	Reflect:	_____
Step 3.	Revise:	_____
Step 4.	Reread:	_____
Step 5.	Record:	_____

5. Sentence 5: **For example, any cook in Ecuador <u>what uses traditional</u> recipes belongs to one of two different regions.**

Which of the following is the best way to write the underlined portion of this sentence? If you think the original is the best way, choose option (1).

(1) what uses traditional

(2) what using traditional

(3) what use traditional

(4) who uses traditional

(5) who use traditional

Step 1.	Read:	_____
Step 2.	Reflect:	_____
Step 3.	Revise:	_____
Step 4.	Reread:	_____
Step 5.	Record:	_____

6. Sentence 6: **The lowlands lie along the Pacific ocean.**

What correction should be made to this sentence?

(1) change *lie* to *lay*
(2) change *lie* to *lies*
(3) insert a comma after *lie*
(4) change *ocean* to *Ocean*
(5) no correction is necessary

Step 1.   Read: _____
Step 2.   Reflect: _____
Step 3.   Revise: _____
Step 4.   Reread: _____
Step 5.   Record: _____

DIRECTIONS: For the next four items, do not write any response to the steps. Simply check each step after you have completed thinking about it. Then circle the correct answer within the test item itself.

7. Sentence 7: **Regional cooks of the lowlands have made great use of <u>fish and seafood, such as lobster shrimp and</u> black conch.**

Which of the following is the best way to write the underlined portion of this sentence? If you think the original is the best way, choose option (1).

(1) fish and seafood, such as lobster shrimp and
(2) fish and seafood, such as lobster, shrimp, and
(3) fish, and seafood, such as lobster, shrimp and
(4) fish and seafood, such as lobster, shrimp, and,
(5) fish and seafood, such as lobster, shrimp and,

Step 1.   _____
Step 2.   _____
Step 3.   _____
Step 4.   _____
Step 5.   _____

8. Sentence 8: **On the other hand, people of the <u>highlands the steep hills</u> surrounding the Andes Mountains, do not have access to fish.**

Which of the following is the best way to write the underlined portion of this sentence? If you think the original is the best way, choose option (1).

(1) highlands the steep hills
(2) highland's, the steep hills
(3) highlands; the steep hills,
(4) highlands; the steep hills
(5) highlands, the steep hills

Step 1.   _____
Step 2.   _____
Step 3.   _____
Step 4.   _____
Step 5.   _____

9. Sentence 9: **They do, however, have potatoes, which are easily grown, stored, and to cook at high altitudes.**

What correction should be made to this sentence?

(1) remove the comma after *do*
(2) change the spelling of *potatoes* to *potatos*
(3) remove the comma after *grown*
(4) change to *cook* to *cooked*
(5) insert a comma after *easily*

Step 1.   _____
Step 2.   _____
Step 3.   _____
Step 4.   _____
Step 5.   _____

10. Sentence 10: **The potato is a major ingredient in ecuadorian highland cooking.**

What correction should be made to this sentence?

(1) change the spelling of *potato* to *potatoe*
(2) change *is* to *are*
(3) change *ecuadorian* to *Ecuadorian*
(4) insert a comma after *ecuadorian*
(5) insert a comma after *highland*

Step 1. _____
Step 2. _____
Step 3. _____
Step 4. _____
Step 5. _____

Answers are on page 87.

Lesson 3   Editing for Correct Usage

DIRECTIONS: As you read the following paragraph, ask yourself the four basic questions that are used when editing for usage. No sentence contains more than one error. Use the 5-R method of editing as you work through each question.

Items 1 to 10 are based on the following paragraph.

(1) The railroad stations of the past is almost extinct. (2) Many stations appeared at a time when few people had drove cars. (3) Before the country's highways were builded, trains were the fastest way to travel long distances. (4) The imposing stations showed the importance of the trains. (5) When New York's Grand Central Station opened, they offered the public an impressive array of services. (6) Barber shops, manicure parlors, restaurants, and a hospital was available to all travelers. (7) In those days, the station even has private baths. (8) However, few of these glamorous services remains in use. (9) Gone are the public's notion of the train as a means of luxurious transportation. (10) Our preference for traveling by airplane and car has hastened the neglect of their train stations.

1. Sentence 1: **The railroad stations of the past <u>is almost extinct.</u>**

Which of the following is the best was to write the underlined portion of this sentence? If you think the original is the best way, choose option (1).

(1) is almost extinct.
(2) are almost extinct.
(3) are almost ekstinct.
(4) is almost ekstinct.
(5) are almost extincts.

2. Sentence 2: **Many stations appeared at a time when <u>few people had drove cars.</u>**

Which of the following is the best way to write the underlined portion of this sentence? If you think the original is the best way, choose option (1).

(1) few people had drove cars
(2) few people drive cars
(3) few people driven cars
(4) few people had drived cars
(5) few people drove cars

3. Sentence 3: **Before the country's highways were builded, trains were the fastest way to travel long distances.**

What correction should be made to this sentence?

(1) change *country's* to *countries*
(2) change *were* to *was*
(3) change *builded* to *built*
(4) remove the comma after *builded*
(5) no correction is necessary

4. Sentence 4: **The imposing stations showed the importance of the trains.**

   If you rewrote sentence 4 beginning with

   The importance of the trains

   the next word should be

   (1) is
   (2) were
   (3) had
   (4) shown
   (5) was

5. Sentence 5: **When New York's Grand Central Station opened, <u>they offered the public</u> an impressive array of services.**

   Which of the following is the best way to write the underlined portion of this sentence? If you think the original is the best way, choose option (1).

   (1) they offered the public
   (2) they offerred the public
   (3) the public offered
   (4) the public was offered
   (5) the public was offerred

6. Sentence 6: **Barber shops, manicure parlors, restaurants, and a hospital was available to all travelers.**

   What correction should be made to this sentence?

   (1) change the spelling of *restaurants* to *restrants*
   (2) change the spelling of *hospital* to *hospitle*
   (3) insert a comma after the word *hospital*
   (4) change *was* to *were*
   (5) change the spelling of *travelers* to *travelors*

7. Sentence 7: **In those days, the <u>station even has</u> private baths.**

   Which of the following is the best way to write the underlined portion of this sentence? If you think the original is the best way, choose option (1).

   (1) station even has
   (2) stations even have
   (3) station's even had
   (4) stations' even have
   (5) station even had

8. Sentence 8: **However, few of these glamorous services remains in use.**

   What corrections should be made to this sentence?

   (1) remove the comma after *however*
   (2) change *these* to *this*
   (3) change *services* to *service*
   (4) change *remains* to *remain*
   (5) no correction is necessary

9. Sentence 9: **<u>Gone are the public's</u> notion of the train as a means of luxurious transportation.**

   Which of the following is the best way to write the underlined portion of this sentence? If you think the original is the best way, choose option (1).

   (1) Gone are the public's
   (2) Gone is the public's
   (3) Gone are, the public's
   (4) Gone is, the public's
   (5) Gone are the publics'

10. Sentence 10: **Our preference for traveling by airplane and car has hastened the neglect of their train stations.**

What correction should be made to this sentence?

(1) change *Our* to *We*
(2) change the spelling of *preference* to *prefrence*
(3) change *has* to *have*
(4) change *their* to *our*
(5) no correction is necessary

Answers are on page 87.

Lesson 4 Editing for Correct Sentence Structure

DIRECTIONS: As you read the following paragraph, ask yourself the four basic questions that are used when editing for sentence structure. No sentence contains more than one error. Use the 5-R method of editing as you work through each question.

Items 1 to 10 are based on the following paragraph.

(1) Many people name the piano as their favorite instrument, in fact, the piano has been the most popular musical instrument for the past two centuries. (2) Capable of simultaneously producing both melody and harmony, musicians prize the piano's versatility. (3) The piano can be played as a solo instrument, as part of an orchestra, or a solo instrument accompanied by an orchestra. (4) Harpsichords are often compared with pianos but have two important limitations. (5) The strings of the harpsichord are plucked piano strings are struck by felt-covered hammers. (6) The loudness of piano music is determined by the touch of the pianist's fingers on the keyboard; as a result, harpsichords have no means by which loudness is controlled. (7) Although there are several types of pianos. (8) The grand piano is the most expensive type, and is found in many concert halls. (9) Grand pianos are usually about nine feet in length. (10) Grand pianos occasionally are built in a smaller size which measures five feet. (11) Because it is more compact in size the vertical piano favored for use in the home.

1. Sentence 1: **Many people name the piano as their favorite instrument, in fact, the piano has been the most popular musical instrument for the past two centuries.**

What correction should be made to this sentence?

(1) insert a comma after *people*
(2) replace the comma after *instrument* with a semicolon
(3) remove the comma after *fact*
(4) insert a comma after *popular*
(5) no correction is necessary

2. Sentence 2: **Capable of simultaneously producing both melody and harmony, musicians prize the piano's versatility.**

Which of the following is the best way to write the underlined portion of this sentence? If you think the original is the best way, choose option (1).

(1) musicians prize the piano's versatility.
(2) musicians prize, the piano's versatility.
(3) the piano's versatility is prized by musicians.
(4) the piano is prized by musicians for its versatility.
(5) the versatility of the piano's is prized by musicians.

3. Sentence 3: **The piano can be played as a solo instrument, as part of an orchestra, or solo instrument accompanied by an orchestra.**

What correction should be made to this sentence?

(1) insert a comma after *played*
(2) remove the comma before *or*
(3) insert the words *as* after *or*
(4) change the spelling of *accompanied* to *acompanied*
(5) no correction is necessary

4. Sentence 4: **Harpsichords are often compared with pianos but have two important limitations.**

If you rewrote sentence 4 beginning with

Although harpsichords are often compared with

the next words should be

(1) pianos, they
(2) pianos, but harpsichords
(3) harpsichords, but pianos
(4) pianos harpsichords
(5) pianos they

5. Sentence 5: **The strings of the harp-sichord are <u>plucked piano</u> strings are struck by felt-covered hammers.**

Which of the following is the best way to write the underlined portion of this sentence? If you think the original is the best way, choose option (1).

(1) plucked piano
(2) plucked, piano
(3) plucked, for instance, piano
(4) plucked, but piano
(5) plucked, so piano

6. Sentence 6: **The loudness of piano music is determined by the touch of the pianist's fingers on the <u>key-board; as a result,</u> harpsichords have no means by which loudness is controlled.**

Which of the following is the best way to write the underlined portion of this sentence? If you think the original is the best way, choose option (1).

(1) keyboard; as a result,
(2) keyboard, as a result
(3) keyboard. As a result
(4) keyboard, because
(5) keyboard; however,

7. Sentence 7: **<u>Although there are several</u> types of pianos.**

Which of the following is the best way to write the underlined portion of this sentence? If you think the original is the best way, choose option (1).

(1) Although there are several
(2) Although there is several
(3) There are several
(4) Although there are sevral
(5) Allthough there are several

8. Sentence 8: **The grand piano is the most expensive type, and is found in many concert halls.**

What correction should be made to this sentence?

(1) capitalize the word *piano*
(2) insert a comma after *piano*
(3) remove the comma after *type*
(4) change *halls* to *hall's*
(5) no correction is necessary

9. Sentences 9 & 10: **Grand pianos are usually about nine feet in length. Grand pianos occasionally are built in a smaller size which measures five feet.**

The most effective combination of sentences 9 and 10 would include which of the following groups of words?

   (1) so they are occasionally
   (2) because they are occasionally
   (3) where they are
   (4) although they occasionally are
   (5) as long as they are

10. Sentence 11: **Because it is more compact in size the vertical piano favored for use in the home.**

Which of the following is the best way to write the underlined portion of this sentence? If you think the original is the best way, choose option (1).

   (1) compact in size the vertical piano favored
   (2) compact. In size the vertical piano is favored
   (3) compact in size. The vertical piano is favored
   (4) compact, in size, the vertical piano is favored
   (5) compact in size, the vertical piano is favored

Answers are on pages 87–88.

Lesson 5 Editing for Mechanical Correction

DIRECTIONS: As you read the following paragraph, ask yourself the four basic questions that are used when editing for mechanical errors. No sentence contains more than one error. Use the 5-R method of editing as you work through each question.

Items 1 to 10 are based on the following paragraph.

(1) The term, poultry refers to the species of birds that are raised for meat and eggs. (2) In some countries', people eat peacock meat. (3) Chicken, turkey, duck, and, goose are popular American poultry. (4) Among these birds, chickens are the most important because they're a source of both meat and eggs. (5) Every year, each american eats an average of 41 pounds of chicken meat and 285 eggs. (6) There are more than 200 variaties of chickens. (7) Duck eggs are more popular in some European Countries than they are in the United States. (8) Geese are much larger than ducks but both species are water birds. (9) Most turkeys raised in the United States are sold at thanksgiving. (10) About half the farmers in America raise poultry on there farms.

1. Sentence 1: **The term, poultry refers to the species of birds that are raised for meat and eggs.**

What correction should be made to this sentence?

   (1) remove the comma after *term*
   (2) insert a comma after *poultry*
   (3) insert a comma after *birds*
   (4) change the spelling of *raised* to *razed*
   (5) no correction is necessary

2. Sentence 2: **In some <u>countries', people eat</u> peacock meat.**

Which of the following is the best way to write the underlined portion of this sentence? If you think the original is the best way, choose option (1).

(1) countries', people eat
(2) country's, people eat
(3) countries, people eat
(4) countrys, people eat
(5) countries', people eats

3. Sentence 3: **Chicken, turkey, duck, and, goose are popular American poultry.**

What correction should be made to this sentence?

(1) Remove the comma after *duck*
(2) Remove the comma after *and*
(3) insert a comma after *goose*
(4) capitalize the word *poultry*
(5) no correction is necessary

4. Sentence 4: **Among these birds, chickens are the most important because they're a source of both meat and eggs.**

What correction should be made to this sentence?

(1) change the spelling of *Among* to *Amung*
(2) replace *these* with *this*
(3) insert a comma after *meat*
(4) replace *they're* with *their*
(5) no correction is necessary

5. Sentence 5: **Every <u>year, each american eats</u> an average of 41 pounds of chicken meat and 285 eggs.**

Which of the following is the best way to write the underlined portion of this sentence? If you think the original is the best way, choose option (1).

(1) year, each american eats
(2) years, each american eats
(3) year, each american eat
(4) year, each ameracan eats
(5) year, each American eats

6. Sentence 6: **There are more than 200 variaties of chickens.**

What correction should be made to this sentence?

(1) replace *There* with *They're*
(2) replace *are* with *is*
(3) replace *than* with *then*
(4) change the spelling of *variaties* to *varieties*
(5) no correction is necessary

7. Sentence 7: **Duck eggs are more popular in some European Countries than they are in the United States.**

What correction should be made to this sentence?

(1) insert a comma after *popular*
(2) change *European* to *european*
(3) change *Countries* to *countries*
(4) replace *than* with *then*
(5) no correction is necessary

8. Sentence 8: **Geese are much larger than ducks but both species are water birds.**

Which of the following is the best way to write the underlined portion of this sentence? If you think the original is the best way, choose option (1).

(1) than ducks but
(2) then ducks but
(3) than ducks, but
(4) than duck's but
(5) than ducks', but

9. Sentence 9: **Most turkeys raised in the United States are sold at thanksgiving.**

What correction should be made to this sentence?

(1) change *turkeys* to *turkies*
(2) insert a comma after *turkeys*
(3) change the spelling of *raised* to *razed*
(4) insert a comma after *States*
(5) change *thanksgiving* to *Thanksgiving*

10. Sentence 10: **About half the farmers in America raise poultry on there farms.**

Which of the following is the best way to write the underlined portion of this sentence? If you think the original is the best way, choose option (1).

(1) poultry on there farms
(2) poultry, on there farms
(3) poultry on there farm's
(4) poultry on their farms
(5) poultry on they're farms

Answers are on page 88.

Lesson 6   Editing Paragraphs

DIRECTIONS: Read the following paragraph and answer the questions that follow by circling the number of the one best answer for each question.

(1) Almost everybody in the world have seen or touched a piece of paper. (2) As we know paper, before the nineteenth century it did not exist. (3) For centuries, cloth rags had been the main chief raw material in paper. (4) Rag paper is still used for fine, expensive writing paper. (5) Vegetable fibers from flax and hemp were treated to form a solid surface, finally, wood pulp was discovered to be a valuable raw material. (6) In 1869, the first mass-production of a paper product, the bag, begins. (7) Today, paper is made into an endless number of products what vary from roofing paper to egg cartons. (8) Paper has dramatically altered the spread of knowledge and information. (9) Books, magazines, and newspapers are available to all at low cost. (10) The production of paper is primarily concentrated in areas that have abundant wood resources. (11) The United states and Canada lead the world in paper production.

1. Sentence 1: **Almost everybody in the world have seen or touched a piece of paper.**

What correction should be made to this sentence?

(1) replace *everybody* with *anybody*
(2) change *have* to *has*
(3) insert a comma after *seen*
(4) change the spelling of *piece* to *peice*
(5) no correction is necessary

2. Sentence 2: **As we know paper, before the nineteenth century it did not exist.**

If you rewrote sentence 2 beginning with

Paper, as we know it,

the next word should be

(1) existed
(2) the
(3) before
(4) did
(5) not

3. Sentence 3: **For centuries, cloth rags had been the main chief raw material in paper.**

What correction should be made to this sentence?

(1) change *centuries* to *centurys*
(2) remove the word *chief*
(3) change *had been* to *are*
(4) insert a comma after *material*
(5) no correction is necessary

4. Sentence 4: **Rag paper is still <u>used for fine, expensive</u> writing paper.**

Which of the following is the best way to write the underlined portion of this sentence? If you think the original is the best way, choose option (1)

(1) used for fine, expensive
(2) used, for fine, expensive
(3) used for, fine, expensive
(4) used for fine expensive
(5) used for fine, expansive

5. Sentence 5: **Vegetable fibers from flax and hemp were treated to form a solid <u>surface, finally, wood pulp</u> was discovered to be a valuable raw material.**

Which of the following is the best way to write the underlined portion of this sentence? If you think the original is the best way, choose option (1).

(1) surface, finally, wood pulp
(2) surface finally, wood pulp
(3) surface. Finally, wood pulp
(4) surface; finally wood pulp
(5) surface, finally, wood pulp

6. Sentence 6: **In 1869, the first mass-production of a paper product, the bag, begins.**

What correction should be made to this sentence?

(1) remove the comma after *1869*
(2) insert a comma after *mass-production*
(3) remove the comma after *bag*
(4) change *begins* to *began*
(5) change *begins* to *begin*

7. Sentence 7: **Today, paper is made into an endless number of <u>products what vary</u> from roofing paper to egg cartons.**

Which of the following is the best way to write the underlined portion of this sentence? If you think the original is the best way, choose option (1).

(1) products what vary
(2) product what varies
(3) products who vary
(4) products, which varies
(5) products that vary

8. Sentences 8 & 9: **Paper has dramatically altered the spread of knowledge and information. Books, magazines, and newspapers are available to all at low cost.**

If you joined sentences 8 and 9 by adding a transition after the word *information*, the best choice would be

(1) instead
(2) for instance
(3) however
(4) rather
(5) meanwhile

9. Sentence 10: **The production of paper is primarily concentrated in areas that have abundent wood resources.**

What correction should be made to this sentence?

(1) change the spelling of *concentrated* to *consentrated*
(2) insert a comma after *areas*
(3) change the spelling of *abundent* to *abundant*
(4) change *resources* to *resource*
(5) no correction is necessary

10. Sentence 11: **The United states and Canada lead the world in paper production.**

Which of the following is the best way to write the underlined portion of this sentence? If you think the original is the best way, choose option (1).

(1) states and Canada lead
(2) states and Canada leads
(3) states, and Canada, lead
(4) States and Canada leads
(5) States and Canada lead

Answers are on page 88.

Directions: The following items are based on a paragraph that contains numbered sentences. Some of the sentences may contain errors in sentence structure, usage, or mechanics. **A few sentences, however, may be correct as written.** Read the paragraph and then answer the nine to ten items that follow it. For each item, choose the answer that would result in the most effective writing of the sentence or sentences. The best answer must be consistent with the meaning and tone of the rest of the paragraph.

Items 1 to 9 are based on the following paragraph.

(1) Many products come with guarantees. (2) A product guarantee is a written promise, it tells what will be done if something goes wrong with the product. (3) Read the guarantee carefully before buying a product. (4) According to Law, it must tell you four things. (5) First, the guarantee must state who stand behind the product. (6) You need to know weather to call the manufacturer, the dealer, or a service agency to get repairs. (7) Second, telling you how long the product is covered. (8) Third, it must describe what is covered. (9) You may receive a refund for a faulty product or the product may be repaired or replaced. (10) If the guarantee is for repairs, you will want to know who pays for labor and shipping. (11) Finally, the guarantee must describe what you're supposed to do if one has a problem with the product. (12) Once you have made your purchase mail in the registration card right away.

1. Sentence 2: **A product guarantee is a written promise, it tells what will be done if something goes wrong with the product.**

   What correction should be made to this sentence?

   (1) change the spelling of *guarantee* to *garrantee*
   (2) replace *promise, it* with *promise. It*
   (3) replace *it tells* with *they tell*
   (4) insert a comma after *done*
   (5) change *goes* to *go*

2. Sentence 3: **Read the guarantee carefully before buying a product.**

   If you rewrote sentence 3 beginning with

   You should read the guarantee carefully before you

   the next word should be

   (1) buying
   (2) buy
   (3) buys
   (4) produce
   (5) product

3. Sentence 4: **According to Law, it must tell you four things.**

   What correction should be made to this sentence?

   (1) change *Law* to *law*
   (2) replace *it* with *they*
   (3) replace *you* with *one*
   (4) change the spelling of *four* to *for*
   (5) no correction is necessary

4. Sentence 5: **First, the guarantee must state who stand behind the product.**

Which of the following is the best way to write the underlined portion of this sentence? If you think the original is the best way, choose option (1).

(1) must state who stand behind
(2) must have stated who stand behind
(3) must state who stands behind
(4) must state who stood behind
(5) must state, who stand behind

5. Sentence 6: **You need to know weather to call the manufacturer, the dealer, or a service agency to get repairs.**

What correction should be made to this sentence?

(1) replace *You need* with *One needs*
(2) change the spelling of *weather* to *whether*
(3) remove the comma after *manufacturer*
(4) insert *calling* after *or*
(5) change *service agency* to *Service Agency*

6. Sentence 7: **Second, telling you how long the product is covered.**

Which of the following is the best way to write the underlined portion of this sentence? If you think the original is the best way, choose option (1).

(1) telling you
(2) telling one
(3) it must tell you
(4) it must have told you
(5) it must tell one

7. Sentence 9: **You may receive a refund for a faulty product or the product may be repaired or replaced.**

Which of the following is the best way to write the underlined portion of this sentence? If you think the original is the best way, choose option (1).

(1) product or the product
(2) product; or the product
(3) product. Or the product
(4) product, or the product
(5) product or, the product

8. Sentence 11: **Finally, the guarantee must describe what you're supposed to do if one has a problem with the product.**

What correction should be made to this sentence?

(1) replace *you're* with *your*
(2) replace *do if* with *do. If*
(3) replace *one* with *you*
(4) change *one has* to *you have*
(5) insert a comma after *problem*

9. Sentence 12: **Once you have made your purchase mail in the registration card right away.**

Which of the following is the best way to write the underlined portion of this sentence? If you think the original is the best way, choose option (1).

(1) have made your purchase mail
(2) made your purchase mail
(3) make your purchase mail
(4) have made your purchase, mail
(5) have made you're purchase, mail

Items 10 to 19 are based on the following paragraph.

(1) There is many ways to acquire job skills. (2) The Armed Forces, for example, offer job training. (3) In addition to job training, the military provides work experience for many jobs. (4) A new recruit whom we'll call Fred Smith, is given interest and ability tests; when he joins the Navy. (5) The tests may indicate that he would make a good cook. (6) In addition to tuition, students at cooking schools have to pay for room and board. (7) If they become dissatisfied, one can drop out or switch schools. (8) Smith is paid while he learns cooking skills, and is expected to spend a certain amount of time in the Navy. (9) When his tour of duty is over, Seaman Smith may choose a military career. (10) If not, he may decide to use the skills he now had to get a job in a restaurant. (11) Maybe deciding on a totally new career. (12) In that case, he can use his veteran's benefits to help pay for returning to school.

10. Sentence 1: **There is many ways to acquire job skills.**

What correction should be made to this sentence?

(1) replace *There* with *Their*
(2) change *is* to *are*
(3) insert *very* after *is*
(4) insert a comma after *ways*
(5) change the spelling of *acquire* to *aquire*

11. Sentences 2 & 3: **The Armed Forces, for example, offer job training. In addition to job training, the military provides work experience for many jobs.**

The most effective combination of sentences 2 and 3 would include which of the following groups of words?

(1) training and in addition to job
(2) offer job training and provides
(3) and the military provides work
(4) in addition it provides work
(5) offer training and work experience

12. Sentence 4: **A new recruit, whom we'll call Fred Smith, is given interest and <u>ability tests; when he joins the Navy.</u>**

Which of the following is the best way to write the underlined portion of this sentence? If you think the original is the best way, choose option (1).

(1) ability tests; when he joins the Navy
(2) ability tests; when he joins the navy
(3) ability tests, when he join the Navy
(4) ability tests when he joins the Navy
(5) ability tests, when joining the Navy

13. Sentence 6: **In addition to tuition, students at cooking schools have to pay for room and board.**

If you rewrote sentence 6 beginning with

Students at cooking schools have to pay for

the next words should be

  (1) tuition, room,
  (2) tuition; room
  (3) room and board,
  (4) room and board.
  (5) additional tuition

14. Sentence 7: **If they become dissatisfied, one can drop out or switch schools.**

Which of the following is the best way to write the underlined portion of this sentence? If you think the original is the best way, choose option (1).

  (1) become dissatisfied, one can
  (2) became dissatisfied they can
  (3) becomes dissatisfied, one can
  (4) become dissatisfied, they can
  (5) become dissatisfied, you can

15. Sentence 8: **Smith is paid while he learns cooking skills, and is expected to spend a certain amount of time in the Navy.**

What correction should be made to this sentence?

  (1) Remove the comma after *skills*
  (2) change *Navy* to *navy*
  (3) change *skills, and* to *skills, but*
  (4) change *is* to *was*
  (5) no correction is necessary

16. Sentence 9: **When his tour of duty is over, Seaman Smith may have chosen a military career.**

What correction should be made to this sentence?

  (1) replace *his* with *his'*
  (2) remove the comma after *over*
  (3) change *Seaman* to *seaman*
  (4) change *have chosen* to *choose*
  (5) change the spelling of *career* to *carreer*

17. Sentence 10: **If not, he may decide to use the skills he now had to get a job in a restaurant.**

What correction should be made to this sentence?

  (1) replace *he may decide* with *deciding*
  (2) change *had* to *has*
  (3) insert a comma after *had*
  (4) replace *to get* with *getting*
  (5) no correction is necessary

18. Sentence 11: **Maybe deciding on a totally new career.**

Which of the following is the best way to write the underlined portion of this sentence? If you think the original is the best way, choose option (1).

  (1) deciding on a totally new
  (2) he decided on a totally new
  (3) he will decide on a totally new
  (4) deciding on a totally, new
  (5) one decides on a totally new

19. Sentence 12: **In that case, he can use his veteran's benefits to help pay for returning to school.**

What correction should be made to this sentence?

(1) replace *he* with *one*
(2) change the spelling of *benefits* to *benifits*
(3) insert a comma after *benefits*
(4) insert *back* after *returning*
(5) no correction is necessary

Items 20 to 28 are based on the following paragraph.

(1) As you have probably noticed, computers are being used in many supermarkets. (2) On many cans and packages are a barcode. (3) The clerk passes the item through a scanner and the group of bars tells what the object is. (4) Some stores even have computers with voices. (5) The voices say the name and price of the item as it passes through the scanner. (6) As the item is rung up, a central computer stores the information that the supermarket now has one less of that item. (7) It takes less time for a clerk to pass your bag of spanish peanuts through a scanner than to type the price into the register. (8) If you're peanuts are from a bin and have no barcode, of course, the scanner can't be used. (9) Still, computerized scales have made the clerk's job easier. (10) All he or she needs to do is put the bag on a scale and typing in the item number. (11) The name, weight, and price of the item were instantly printed on the receipt tape. (12) Computer have made supermarket lines shorter, inventories easier, and prices are lower.

20. Sentence 2: **On many cans and packages are a barcode.**

Which of the following is the best way to write the underlined portion of this sentence? If you think the original is the best way, choose option (1).

(1) cans and packages are a barcode.
(2) cans, and packages are a barcode.
(3) cans and on packages are a barcode.
(4) cans and packages being a barcode.
(5) cans and packages is a barcode.

21. Sentence 3: **The clerk passes the item through a scanner and the group of bars tells what the object is.**

What correction should be made to this sentence?

(1) replace *through* with *threw*
(2) insert a comma after *scanner*
(3) change *tells* to *tell*
(4) change *is* to *was*
(5) no correction is necessary

22. Sentences 4 & 5: **Some stores even have computers with voices. The voices say the name and price of the item as it passes through the scanner.**

The most effective combination of sentences 4 and 5 would include which of the following groups of words?

(1) They even have computers with
(2) with voices that say the name
(3) with voices and the voices say
(4) or the voices say the name and
(5) Some stores even say the name

23. Sentence 6: **As the item is rung up, a central computer stores the information that the supermarket now has one less of that item.**

What correction should be made to this sentence?

(1) change *is* to *was*
(2) remove the comma after *up*
(3) change *stores* to *store*
(4) change *supermarket* to *Supermarket*
(5) no correction is necessary

24. Sentence 7: **It takes less time for a clerk to pass your bag of spanish peanuts through a scanner than to type the price into the register.**

What correction should be made to this sentence?

(1) replace *less* with *lesser*
(2) replace *spanish* with *Spanish*
(3) insert a comma after *scanner*
(4) replace *than* with *as*
(5) replace *to type* with *typing*

25. Sentence 8: **If you're peanuts are from a bin and have no barcode, of course, the scanner can't be used.**

What correction should be made to this sentence?

(1) replace *you're* with *one's*
(2) insert a comma after *bin*
(3) replace *have* with *has*
(4) remove the comma after *barcode*
(5) change the spelling of *you're* to *your*

26. Sentence 10: **All he or she needs to do is put the bag on a scale and typing in the item number.**

What correction should be made to this sentence?

(1) replace *needs* with *need*
(2) replace *is* with *was*
(3) replace *put* with *putting*
(4) insert a comma after *scale*
(5) replace *typing* with *type*

27. Sentence 11: **The name, weight, and price of the item were instantly printed on the receipt tape.**

Which of the following is the best way to write the underlined portion of this sentence? If you think the original is the best way, choose option (1).

(1) weight, and price of the item were
(2) weight and price of the item were
(3) weight, and price of the item are
(4) weight, and price of the item is
(5) weight, and price of the item being

28. Sentence 12: **Computers have made supermarket lines shorter, inventories easier, and prices are lower.**

Which of the following is the best way to write the underlined portion of this sentence? If you think the original is the best way, choose option (1).

(1) easier, and prices are lower.
(2) more easy, and prices are lower.
(3) easier and prices are lower.
(4) easier, and made prices lower.
(5) easier, and prices lower.

Answers are on pages 88–90.

Half-Length Practice Test

Performance Analysis Chart

Directions: Circle the number of each item that you got correct on the Half-length Practice Test. Count how many items you got correct in each row; count how many items you got correct in each column. Write the amount correct per row and column as the numerator in the fraction in the appropriate "Total Correct" box. (The denominators represent the total number of items in the row or column.) Write the grand total correct over the denominator **28** at the lower right corner of the chart. (For example, if you got 24 items correct, write *24* so that the fraction reads 24/**28**.)

Item Type	Usage (Chapter 1)	Sentence Structure (Chapter 2)	Mechanics (Chapter 3)	TOTAL CORRECT
Construction Shift	2	11, 22	13	/4
Sentence Correction	8, 10, 16, 17, 23	1, 21, 26	3, 5, 15, 19, 24, 25	/14
Sentence Revision	4, 14, 20, 27	6, 7, 12, 18, 28	9	/10
TOTAL CORRECT	/10	/10	/8	/28

The Unit I chapters named in parentheses indicate where in the Writing Skills instruction of the *New Revised Cambridge GED Program: Comprehensive Book* you can find specific instruction about the areas of grammar you encountered on the Half-length Practice Test. You can find more in-depth instruction in the *New Revised Cambridge GED Program: Writing Skills.*

On the chart, items are classified as Construction Shift, Sentence Correction, and Sentence Revision. These three item types are introduced in the *New Revised Cambridge GED Program: Comprehensive Book* and the *New Revised Cambridge GED Program: Writing Skills.*

Full-Length Practice Test

Directions: The following items are based on a paragraph that contains numbered sentences. Some of the sentences may contain errors in sentence structure, usage, or mechanics. A few sentences, however, may be correct as written. Read the paragraph and then answer the nine to ten items that follow it. For each item, choose the answer that would result in the most effective writing of the sentence or sentences. The best answer must be consistent with the meaning and tone of the rest of the paragraph.

Items 1 to 9 are based on the following paragraph.

(1) Penicillin, a prescription medicine, has certainly improved our lives. (2) It was discovered in 1928 by dr. Alexander Fleming. (3) Who had been growing bacteria in a dish as an experiment. (4) Returning one day to his laboratory, something interesting was noticed. (5) Some mold from outdoors had blown in and killed most of the bacteria. (6) Dr. Fleming took this and made penicillin from it. (7) He found that penicillin could be used to treat infections caused by bacteria. (8) As a result of this discovery many illnesses are now easily cured. (9) Its important to remember that neither penicillin nor any other drug is to be taken carelessly. (10) Penicillin doesn't cure everything, and was the cause of some allergic reactions. (11) If you get sick, let you're doctor decide if you need penicillin; never take it on your own. (12) After taking penicillin, you watched carefully for any signs of allergy, such as itching or shortness of breath.

1. Sentence 2: **It was discovered in 1928 by dr. Alexander Fleming.**

   What correction should be made to this sentence?

   (1) change *was* to *is*
   (2) change the spelling of *discovered* to *diskovered*
   (3) insert a comma after *1928*
   (4) change *dr.* to *Dr.*
   (5) no correction is necessary

2. Sentence 3: **Who had been growing bacteria in a dish as an experiment.**

   What correction should be made to this sentence?

   (1) replace *Who* with *He*
   (2) change *had* to *has*
   (3) insert a comma after *dish*
   (4) replace *as* with *of*
   (5) no correction is necessary

3. Sentence 4: **Returning one day to his laboratory, something interesting was noticed.**

   Which of the following is the best way to write the underlined portion of this sentence? If you think the original is the best way, choose option (1).

   (1) laboratory, something interesting was noticed.
   (2) laboratory. Something interesting was noticed.
   (3) laboratory; something interesting was noticed.
   (4) laboratory he noticed something interesting.
   (5) laboratory, he noticed something interesting

4. Sentence 6: **Dr. Fleming took this and made penicillin from it.**

   If you rewrote sentence 6 beginning with

   Dr. Fleming made

   the next word should be

   (1) taking
   (2) and
   (3) penicillin
   (4) mold
   (5) it

5. Sentence 8: **As a result of this discovery many illnesses are now easily cured.**

   Which of the following is the best way to write the underlined portion of this sentence? If you think the original is the best way, choose option (1).

   (1) As a result of this discovery
   (2) Resulting from this discovery
   (3) Caused by this discovery
   (4) As a result of this discovery,
   (5) As a result of this discovery;

6. Sentence 9: **Its important to remember that neither penicillin nor any other drug is to be taken carelessly.**

   What correction should be made to this sentence?

   (1) change *is* to *are*
   (2) change *is* to *was*
   (3) replace *penicillin* with *Penicillin*
   (4) change *Its* to *It's*
   (5) insert a comma before *nor*

7. Sentence 10: **Penicillin doesn't cure everything, and was the cause of some allergic reactions.**

   What correction should be made to this sentence?

   (1) change the spelling of *doesn't* to *dosn't*
   (2) remove the comma after *everything*
   (3) replace *everything, and* with *everything. And*
   (4) replace *and* with *but*
   (5) replace *was the cause of some* with *it can cause some*

8. Sentence 11: **If you get sick, let you're doctor decide if you need penicillin; never take it on your own.**

   What correction should be made to this sentence?

   (1) replace *you're* with *your*
   (2) change *doctor* to *Doctor*
   (3) change *need* to *needed*
   (4) replace *penicillin;* with *penicillin so*
   (5) replace *your* with *you're*

9. Sentence 12: **After taking penicillin, you watched carefully for any signs of allergy, such as itching or shortness of breath.**

   Which of the following is the best way to write the underlined portion of this sentence? If you think the original is the best way, choose option (1).

   (1) penicillin, you watched carefully
   (2) penicillin, you should watch carefully
   (3) penicillin; you watched carefully
   (4) penicillin you watched, carefully
   (5) penicillin, one watches carefully

Items 10 to 19 are based on the following paragraph

(1) Anyone who is beginning a job training program in this day and age today is learning something. (2) He or she soon discovers that each occupation has its own technical language. (3) An air conditioning mechanic probably knows more than anyone else about the names for various parts of an air conditioner. (4) An account clerk, which is responsible for recording sales figures, needs to learn financial terms. (5) Drafters often have to discuss designs of machines they've drew. (6) A machine tool operator cuts and shapes metal, and he or she needs to be able to talk about his or her machine. (7) A welder, like a machine tool operator, works with metal. (8) The welder learns words that describe the process of joining pieces of hot metal. (9) Medical secretaries and nurses both needing to know the names of medications and medical procedures. (10) When you end a training program; you do not stop learning special vocabulary. (11) One will learn a lot of technical vocabulary while on the job.

10. Sentences 1 & 2: **Anyone who is beginning a job training program in this day and age today is learning something. He or she soon discovers that each occupation has its own technical language.**

The most effective combination of sentences 1 and 2 would include which of the following groups of words?

(1) He or she is beginning to soon discover
(2) Anyone soon discovers that
(3) Anyone in this day and age discovers
(4) begins a job training program today soon
(5) day and age today soon learns about

11. Sentence 3: **An air conditioning mechanic probably knows more than anyone else about the names for various parts of an air conditioner.**

What correction should be made to this sentence?

(1) change *mechanic* to *Mechanic*
(2) replace *than anyone else* with *as anyone*
(3) insert a comma after *anyone*
(4) change the spelling of *conditioner* to *conditionner*
(5) no correction is necessary

12. Sentence 4: **An account clerk, which is responsible for recording sales figures, needs to learn financial terms.**

What correction should be made to this sentence?

(1) change *account clerk* to *Account Clerk*
(2) replace *which* with *who*
(3) change the spelling of *for* to *four*
(4) replace *figures, needs* with *figures; needs*
(5) change *needs* to *need*

13. Sentence 5: **Drafters often have to discuss designs of machines they've drew.**

What correction should be made to this sentence?

(1) change *have* to *had*
(2) replace *often have* with *have often*
(3) change the spelling of *they've* to *the've*
(4) insert a comma after *machines*
(5) change *drew* to *drawn*

14. Sentence 6: **A machine tool operator cuts and shapes metal, and he or she needs to be able to talk about his or her machine.**

If you rewrote sentence 6 beginning with

A machine tool operator, who cuts and shapes metal,

the next word should be

- **(1)** and
- **(2)** he
- **(3)** they
- **(4)** needs
- **(5)** talks

15. Sentence 7: **A welder, like a machine tool <u>operator, works with metal.</u>**

Which of the following is the best way to write the underlined portion of this sentence? If you think the original is the best way, choose option (1).

- **(1)** operator, works with metal.
- **(2)** operator works with metal.
- **(3)** operator work with metal.
- **(4)** operator working with metal.
- **(5)** operator, work with metal.

16. Sentence 8: **The welder learns words that describe the process of joining pieces of hot metal.**

What correction should be made to this sentence?

- **(1)** replace *that* with *who*
- **(2)** change the spelling of *describe* to *discribe*
- **(3)** insert a comma after *process*
- **(4)** change the spelling of *pieces* to *peaces*
- **(5)** no correction is necessary

17. Sentence 9: **Medical secretaries and nurses both needing to know the names of medications and medical procedures.**

What correction should be made to this sentence?

- **(1)** change the spelling of *secretaries* to *secrataries*
- **(2)** change *needing* to *need*
- **(3)** replace *know the names* with *know; the names*
- **(4)** insert a comma after *medications*
- **(5)** change the spelling of *procedures* to *proceedures*

18. Sentence 10: **When you end a training <u>program; you do not stop</u> learning special vocabulary.**

Which of the following is the best way to write the underlined portion of this sentence? If you think the original is the best way, choose option (1).

- **(1)** program; you do not stop
- **(2)** program, you do not stop
- **(3)** program. You do not stop
- **(4)** program you do not stop
- **(5)** program; one does not stop

19. Sentence 11: **One will learn a lot of technical vocabulary while on the job.**

What correction needs to be made to this sentence?

- **(1)** replace *One* with *You*
- **(2)** replace *will learn* with *learned*
- **(3)** insert a comma after *vocabulary*
- **(4)** insert *one was* after *while*
- **(5)** no correction is necessary

Items 20 to 28 are based on the following paragraph.

(1) There is few businesses today that do not use computers. (2) Although companies are trying to make profits, it's important for any company to keep track of its money. (3) Computers those gifts of modern science, are ideal for storing financial information. (4) Let's consider an imaginary stationery supply company, for example. (5) Suppose I need a typewriter ribbon that a company called Jones Halo makes. (6) Neither the local office supply store nor the one in the next town have the ribbon. (7) The day after Valentine's day, I send an order form and a check to the company's mail order department in Barley, New York. (8) Someone their receives my order and types the information into a computer. (9) The ribbons are shipped east to my home at 20 Tinker Street in Woodstock, New York. (10) On the last day of February, a delivery person brings me the package. (11) Taped to the flaps of the box is a computer-made copy of the invoice listing, items, item numbers, and, prices. (12) All of this information, as well as records of millions of other sales, has been neatly stored in a computer at Jones Halo.

20. Sentence 1: **There is few businesses today that do not use computers.**

    Which of the following is the best way to write the underlined portion of this sentence? If you think the original is the best way, choose option (1).

    (1) There is few businesses today that
    (2) Today, there is few businesses that
    (3) There is few businesses today, that
    (4) There is few businesses today who
    (5) There are few businesses today that

21. Sentence 2: **Although companies are trying to make profits, it's important for any company to keep track of its money.**

    What correction should be made to this sentence?

    (1) replace *Although* with *Because*
    (2) replace *companies* with *company's*
    (3) replace *it's* with *its*
    (4) replace *any company* with *it*
    (5) replace *its* with *it's*

22. Sentence 3: **Computers those gifts of modern science, are ideal for storing financial information.**

    What correction should be made to this sentence?

    (1) insert a comma after *Computers*
    (2) change *science* to *Science*
    (3) remove the comma after *science*
    (4) change *are* to *is*
    (5) no correction is necessary

23. Sentence 5: **Suppose I need a typewriter ribbon that a company called Jones Halo makes.**

    If you rewrote sentence 5 beginning with

    Suppose I need a typewriter ribbon made

    the next word should be

    (1) that
    (2) the
    (3) by
    (4) so
    (5) for

24. Sentence 6: **Neither the local office supply store nor the <u>one in the next town have</u> the ribbon.**

Which of the following is the best way to write the underlined portion of this sentence? If you think the original is the best way, choose option (1).

   (1) one in the next town have
   (2) one in the next town has
   (3) one in the next town, have
   (4) next town's one have
   (5) one in the next neighboring town have

25. Sentence 7: **The day after Valentine's day, I sent an order form and a check to the company's mail order department in Barley, New York.**

What correction should be made to this sentence?

   (1) change *day* to *Day*
   (2) remove the comma after *day*
   (3) replace *check to* with *check. To*
   (4) change *company's* to *Company's*
   (5) change *Barley* to *barley*

26. Sentence 8: **Someone their receives my order and types the information into a computer.**

What correction should be made to this sentence?

   (1) replace *their* with *there*
   (2) change *receives* to *receiving*
   (3) insert a comma after *order*
   (4) replace *order and* with *order. One*
   (5) change *types* to *typed*

27. Sentence 9: **The ribbons are shipped east to my home at 20 Tinker Street in Woodstock, New York.**

What correction should be made to this sentence?

   (1) replace *ribbons* with *ribbon's*
   (2) change *are* to *were*
   (3) change *east* to *East*
   (4) change *Street* to *street*
   (5) no correction is necessary

28. Sentence 11: **Taped to the flaps of the box is a computer-made copy of the invoice <u>listing, items, item numbers, and, prices.</u>**

Which of the following is the best way to write the underlined portion of this sentence? If you think the original is the best way, choose option (1).

   (1) listing, items, item numbers, and, prices
   (2) listing items, item numbers, and, prices
   (3) listing, items, item numbers, and prices
   (4) listing items, item, numbers, and prices
   (5) listing items, item numbers, and prices

Items 29 to 37 are based on the following paragraph.

(1) If you're planning on buying a house and you'll probably need a loan. (2) The government offers several mortgage plans one of these is the Federal Housing Administration mortgage. (3) If you meet the requirements for an FHA loan, Uncle Sam will help you reduce your house payments. (4) With an FHA loan, the down payment and each monthly payment is usually less than for other loans. (5) In other words, you pay less at the start and smaller monthly checks. (6) It is not always easy to get an FHA loan. (7) Not surprisingly, the government wants to make sure your someone who will repay the loan. (8) You might be one of the people with a poor credit rating, for instance. (9) They may not be able to get one. (10) If you do get one, you will be expected to pay interest. (11) The interest will be fairly low but the rate changes. (12) To find out how high the rate has rose, write to the FHA in Washington, D.C.

29. Sentence 1: **If you're planning on buying a <u>house and you'll probably need</u> a loan.**

Which of the following is the best way to write the underlined portion of this sentence? If you think the original is the best way, choose option (1).

- **(1)** house and you'll probably need
- **(2)** house, and you'll probably need
- **(3)** house, you'll probably need
- **(4)** house you'll probably need
- **(5)** house, one will probably need

30. Sentence 2: **The government offers several mortgage <u>plans one of these is</u> the Federal Housing Administration mortgage.**

Which of the following is the best way to write the underlined portion of this sentence? If you think the original is the best way, choose option (1).

- **(1)** plans one of these is
- **(2)** plans. One of these is
- **(3)** plans because one of these is
- **(4)** plans, one of these is
- **(5)** plans one of these are

31. Sentence 3: **If you meet the requirements for an FHA loan, Uncle Sam will help you reduce your house payments.**

What correction should be made to this sentence?

- **(1)** replace *you meet* with *one meets*
- **(2)** change the spelling of *requirements* to *requirments*
- **(3)** remove the comma after *loan*
- **(4)** change *Uncle* to *uncle*
- **(5)** no correction is necessary

32. Sentence 4: **With an FHA loan, the down payment and each monthly <u>payment is usually less than for</u> other loans.**

Which of the following is the best way to write the underlined portion of this sentence? If you think the original is the best way, choose option (1).

- **(1)** payment is usually less than for
- **(2)** payment are usually less than for
- **(3)** payment is usually less than
- **(4)** payment, are usually less than for
- **(5)** payment is usually less, than for

33. Sentence 5: **In other words, you pay less at the start and smaller monthly checks.**

What correction should be made to this sentence?

(1) replace *pay* with *paid*
(2) insert a comma after *start*
(3) insert *more* after *and*
(4) replace *start and* with *start, and you write*
(5) change *monthly* to *Monthly*

34. Sentence 7: **Not surprisingly, the government wants to make sure your someone who will repay the loan.**

What correction should be made to this sentence?

(1) insert a comma after *who*
(2) remove the comma after *surprisingly*
(3) change the spelling of *government* to *goverment*
(4) change the spelling of *your* to *you're*
(5) replace *who* with *which*

35. Sentences 8 & 9: **You might be one of the people with a poor credit rating, for instance. They may not be able to get one.**

The most effective combination of sentences 8 and 9 would include which of the following groups of words?

(1) If you are one of those with a poor one,
(2) Suppose one has a poor credit rating,
(3) you may not be able to get one.
(4) so he may not be able to get it.
(5) who may not be able

36. Sentence 11: **The interest will be fairly <u>low but the rate changes.</u>**

Which of the following is the best way to write the underlined portion of this sentence? If you think the original is the best way, choose option (1).

(1) low but the rate changes.
(2) low. But the rate changes.
(3) low; but the rate changes.
(4) low, but the rate changes.
(5) low but it changes.

37. Sentence 12: **To find out how high the rate has rose, write to the FHA in Washington, D.C.**

What correction should be made to this sentence?

(1) insert *up* after *high*
(2) change *has rose* to *has risen*
(3) change the spelling of *write* to *right*
(4) change *Washington* to *washington*
(5) no correction is necessary

Items 38 to 46 are based on the following paragraph.

(1) What is data processing? (2) Data processors all did some kind of computer work. (3) Some data processors type information on a keyboard linked to a computer; and others run the computer, itself. (4) There are many different data processing jobs. (5) There are also many different programs offering training. (6) Some Companies will pay you while you are being trained. (7) Such company training programs are highly desireable and attract many applicants. (8) Often, filling out the application form requires a lot of time, effort, and being accurate. (9) The form tests your ability to follow directions, an essential one for data processors. (10) If one can't get into a company training program, don't worry. (11) Those who have their equivalency diplomas will find one. (12) Even if you have to work for a summer or two to earn money for community college or technical school. (13) Time spent working is not wasted, though, because the experience may help get you into the program you want.

38. Sentence 2: **Data processors <u>all did some kind of</u> computer work.**

Which of the following is the best way to write the underlined portion of this sentence? If you think the original is the best way, choose option (1).

(1) all did some kind of
(2) all do some kind of
(3) all does some kind of
(4) all done some kind of
(5) all did some kind, of

39. Sentence 3: **Some data processors type information on a keyboard linked to a <u>computer; and others run the computer,</u> itself.**

Which of the following is the best way to write the underlined portion of this sentence? If you think the original is the best way, choose option (1).

(1) computer; and others run the computer,
(2) computer; others running the computer
(3) computer; and others run the computer
(4) computer; others run the computer
(5) computer. And others run the computer

40. Sentences 4 & 5: **There are many different data processing jobs. There are also many different programs offering training.**

The most effective combination of sentences 4 and 5 would include which of the following groups of words?

(1) jobs but also many
(2) Not only are many different data
(3) for there are also many
(4) and also many different programs
(5) and training programs.

41. Sentence 6: **Some Companies will pay you while you are being trained.**

What correction should be made to this sentence?

(1) change *Companies* to *companies*
(2) change *will pay* to *would have paid*
(3) replace *while* with *at the same time as*
(4) replace *you are* with *one is*
(5) no correction is necessary

42. Sentence 7: **Such company training programs are highly desireable and attract many applicants.**

What correction should be made to this sentence?

(1) insert *very* after *are*
(2) change the spelling of *desireable* to *desirable*
(3) insert a comma after *desireable*
(4) change *attract* to *attracts*
(5) no correction is necessary

43. Sentence 8: **Often, filling out the application form requires a lot of time, effort, and being accurate.**

Which of the following is the best way to write the underlined portion of this sentence? If you think the original is the best way, choose option (1).

(1) time, effort, and being accurate.
(2) time, effort, and accuracy.
(3) time, effort, and your being accurate.
(4) time, effort and being accurate.
(5) time, making effort, and being accurate.

44. Sentence 9: **The form tests your ability to follow directions, an essential one for data processors.**

What correction should be made to this sentence?

(1) replace *your* with *you're*
(2) remove the comma after *directions*
(3) change the spelling of *essential* to *essencial*
(4) replace *one* with *skill*
(5) replace *processors* with *processors'*

45. Sentence 10: **If one can't get into a company training program, don't worry.**

Which of the following is the best way to write the underlined portion of this sentence? If you think the original is the best way, choose option (1).

(1) If one can't get
(2) If you can't get
(3) Even supposing one can't get
(4) If in the event one can't get
(5) Because one can't get

46. Sentence 11: **Those who have their equivalency diplomas will find one.**

If you rewrote sentence 11 beginning with

As long as you have your equivalency diploma,

the next word should be

(1) you
(2) those
(3) their
(4) one
(5) a

47. Sentence 12: **Even if you have to work for a summer or two to earn money for community college or technical school.**

What correction should be made to this sentence?

(1) replace *Even if you* with *You may*
(2) change *summer* to *Summer*
(3) insert a comma after *money*
(4) change *money for* to *money. For*
(5) change *community college* to *Community College*

Items 48 to 55 are based on the following paragraph.

(1) You may hear someone say that computers don't ever make mistakes on their own but that isn't quite true. (2) People are responsible for most computer errors, but computers do sometimes cause the problems. (3) Inside a computer is many electronic parts, and a problem with any one of them can have a disastrous effect. (4) Many of the miniature parts that contain the computer's memory are made in japan. (5) Suppose they pack one of these chips very carefully and ship it to the U.S., where it becomes part of a computer. (6) Later, the person writing instructions for the computer keeps getting the wrong answers from the computer. (7) Should we blame the Japanese part or the American programmer? (8) Maybe neither is at fault; a Canadian air mass bringing a summer storm may be to blame. (9) Weather, as well as the people who work with a computer, sometimes caused important information to be lost. (10) For this reason, a group of copies, called backup files, is often made and put into a fireproof safe. (11) That way, even if lightning or a fire damages the computer, copies of the information remain on tape.

48. Sentence 1: **You may hear someone say that computers don't ever make mistakes on their own but that isn't quite true.**

What correction should be made to this sentence?

(1) change the spelling of *hear* to *here*
(2) replace *their* with *they're*
(3) insert a comma after *own*
(4) replace *isn't* with *wasn't*
(5) change the spelling of *quite* to *quiet*

49. Sentence 2: **People are responsible for most computer errors, but computers do sometimes cause the problems.**

If you rewrote sentence 2 beginning with

Although people are responsible for most computer errors,

the next word should be

(1) but
(2) still
(3) and
(4) they
(5) computers

50. Sentence 3: **Inside a computer is many electronic parts, and a problem with any one of them can have a disastrous effect.**

Which of the following is the best way to write the underlined portion of this sentence? If you think the original is the best way, choose option (1).

(1) is many electronic parts, and
(2) is many electronic parts and
(3) is many electronic parts; and
(4) are many electronic parts, and
(5) are many electronic parts and

51. Sentence 4: **Many of the miniature parts that contain the computer's memory are made in japan.**

What correction should be made to this sentence?

(1) change the spelling of *miniature* to *miniataur*
(2) change *contain* to *contains*
(3) insert a comma after *memory*
(4) change *are* to *is*
(5) change *japan* to *Japan*

52. Sentence 5: **Suppose <u>they pack one of these chips very carefully and ship it</u> to the U.S., where it becomes part of a computer.**

Which of the following is the best way to write the underlined portion of this sentence? If you think the original is the best way, choose option (1).

(1) they pack one of these chips very carefully and ship
(2) they pack one of these chips very careful and ship
(3) they carefully pack one of these chips and ship
(4) one of these chips is packed very carefully and shipped
(5) one of these chips is packed and very carefully shipped

53. Sentence 8: **Maybe neither is at fault; a Canadian air mass bringing a summer storm may be to blame.**

What correction should be made to this sentence?

(1) change *is* to *are*
(2) replace *fault; a* with *fault a*
(3) change *Canadian* to *canadian*
(4) change *summer* to *Summer*
(5) no correction is necessary

54. Sentence 9: **Weather, as well as the people who work with a computer, sometimes caused important information to be lost.**

What correction should be made to this sentence?

(1) replace *the people* with *one*
(2) remove the comma after *computer*
(3) change *caused* to *cause*
(4) change *caused* to *causes*
(5) no correction is necessary

55. Sentence 10: **For this reason, a group of copies, called backup files, <u>is often made and put</u> into a fireproof safe.**

Which of the following is the best way to write the underlined portion of this sentence? If you think the original is the best way, choose option (1).

(1) is often made and put
(2) is often made and are put
(3) are often made and put
(4) often being made and put
(5) had often been made and put

Answers are on pages 90–92.

Full-Length Practice Test

Performance Analysis Chart

Directions: Circle the number of each item that you got correct on the Full-length Practice Test. Count how many items you got correct in each row; count how many items you got correct in each column. Write the amount correct per row and column as the numerator in the fraction in the appropriate "Total Correct" box. (The denominators represent the total number of items in the row or column.) Write the grand total correct over the denominator **55** at the lower right corner of the chart. (For example, if you got 50 items correct, write *50* so that the fraction reads 50/**55**.)

Item Type	Usage (Chapter 1)	Sentence Structure (Chapter 2)	Mechanics (Chapter 3)	TOTAL CORRECT
Construction Shift	4, 46	10, 23, 35, 40, 49	14	/8
Sentence Correction	7, 11, 12, 13, 19, 37, 44, 54	2, 17, 21, 33, 47, 48, 53	1, 6, 8, 16, 22, 25, 26, 27, 31, 34, 41, 42, 51	/28
Sentence Revision	9, 15, 20, 24, 32, 38, 45, 52, 55	3, 29, 30, 36, 39, 43, 50	5, 18, 28	/19
TOTAL CORRECT	/19	/19	/17	/55

The Unit I chapters named in parentheses indicate where in the Writing Skills instruction of the *New Revised Cambridge GED Program: Comprehensive Book* you can find specific instruction about the areas of grammar you encountered on the Full-length Practice Test. You can find more in-depth instruction in the *New Revised Cambridge GED Program: Writing Skills*.

On the chart, items are classified as Construction Shift, Sentence Correction, and Sentence Revision. These three item types are introduced in the *New Revised Cambridge GED Program: Comprehensive Book* and the *New Revised Cambridge GED Program: Writing Skills*.

TIME: 75 minutes

DIRECTIONS: The following items are based on a paragraph that contains numbered sentences. Some of the sentences may contain errors in sentence structure, usage, or mechanics. **A few sentences, however, may be correct as written.** Read the paragraph and then answer the eight to ten items that follow it. For each item, choose the answer that would result in the most effective writing of the sentence or sentences. The best answer must be consistent with the meaning and tone of the rest of the paragraph.

Items 1 to 9 are based on the following paragraph.

(1) The U.S. Government Printing Office publishes many booklets of interest to consumers. (2) Some of the booklets are free others cost a dollar or two. (3) The numerous topics covered include careers, hobbies, and nutrition. (4) Several of the publications deal with writing activities. (5) There being one about how to write letters of complaint, for example. (6) There is another for those interested in learning how to record your family history. (7) If you've had difficulty in figuring out how to get copies of vital records. (8) There is a booklet that will help you find where to write for such things as certificates of birth death, marriage, and divorce. (9) If your interested in ordering some of the pamphlets, you may want to see a catalog listing the titles available. (10) To request the catalog, write to: Consumer Information-Z, P.O. Box 100, Pueblo, colorado 81002.

1. Sentence 2: **Some of the booklets are free others cost a dollar or two.**

Which of the following is the best way to write the underlined portion of this sentence? If you think the original is the best way, choose option (1).

(1) Some of the booklets are free others cost a dollar or two.
(2) Some of the booklets is free others cost a dollar or two.
(3) Some of the booklets are free, others cost a dollar or two.
(4) Some of the booklets are free for others cost a dollar or two.
(5) Some of the booklets are free; others cost a dollar or two.

2. Sentence 3: **The numerous topics covered include careers, hobbies, and nutrition.**

If you rewrote sentence 3 beginning with

Careers, hobbies, and nutrition

the next word should be

(1) include
(2) includes
(3) including
(4) are
(5) is

3. Sentence 4: **Several of the publications deal with writing activities.**

Which of the following is the best way to write the underlined portion of this sentence? If you think the original is the best way, choose option (1).

(1) deal with writing activities.
(2) which deal with writing activities.
(3) dealing with writing activities.
(4) dealt with writing activities.
(5) had dealt with writing activities.

4. Sentence 5: **There being one about how to write letters of complaint, for example.**

What correction should be made to this sentence?

(1) replace There with They're
(2) change being to is
(3) change complaint to Complaint
(4) remove the comma after complaint
(5) no correction is necessary

5. Sentence 6: **There is another for those interested in learning how to record your family history.**

What correction should be made to this sentence?

(1) replace There with They're
(2) change is to being
(3) change the spelling of another to an other
(4) insert a comma after how
(5) replace your with their

6. Sentence 7: **If you've had difficulty in figuring out how to get copies of vital records.**

Which of the following is the best way to write the underlined portion of this sentence? If you think the original is the best way, choose option (1).

(1) If you've had difficulty in figuring out
(2) You may have had difficulty in figuring out
(3) You had difficulty in figuring out
(4) If one has had difficulty in figuring out
(5) If you've had difficulty, in figuring out

7. Sentence 8: **There is a booklet that will help you find where to write for such things as certificates of birth death, marriage, and divorce.**

Which of the following is the best way to write the underlined portion of this sentence? If you think the original is the best way, choose option (1).

(1) to write for such things as certificates of birth death,
(2) to have written for such things as certificates of birth death,
(3) to write, for such things as certificates of birth death,
(4) to write for such things as certificates of birth or death,
(5) to write for such things as certificates of birth, death,

8. Sentence 9: **If your interested in ordering some of the pamphlets, you may want to see a catalog listing the titles available.**

What correction should be made to this sentence?

(1) replace your with you're
(2) change the spelling of pamphlets to panphlets
(3) remove the comma after pamphlets
(4) change you to one
(5) change catalog to Catalog

9. Sentence 10: **To request the catalog, write to: Consumer Information-Z, P.O. Box 100, Pueblo, colorado 81002.**

What correction should be made to this sentence?

(1) replace To with Too
(2) change write to writing
(3) replace to: Consumer with to; Consumer
(4) change colorado to Colorado
(5) no correction is necessary

Items 10 to 16 are based on the following paragraph.

(1) Teenagers are more likely than other drivers to be involved in automobile accidents. (2) In fact, their chance of getting into an auto accident is almost three times that of the average driver. (3) Alcohol, as well as speeding, play a central role in many of the car accidents teens have. (4) Driving while drunk unfortunately results in about eleven teens dying each day. (5) It is clear that drunk driving is a serious problem in the United States, however, how to solve the problem is not as obvious. (6) Different states are trying various combinations of solutions. (7) Neither curfews nor educational programs is going to prevent all accidents, but it is hoped that, together, they will reduce the number due to alcohol. (8) Likewise, raising the licensing and drinking ages won't eliminate all car crashes, but such changes might cut down on accidents. (9) After more studies have been done on the effectiveness of each method, it became more apparent which ones are the best. (10) Then perhaps we can find a more consistent way to fight the nation's number one killer of teenagers. (11) That killer is drunk driving accidents.

10. Sentence 3: **Alcohol, as well as speeding, play a central role in many of the car accidents teens have.**

What correction should be made to this sentence?

(1) change play to plays
(2) change the spelling of role to rowl
(3) insert a comma after role
(4) change have to having
(5) no correction is necessary

11. Sentence 4: **Driving while drunk unfortunately results in about eleven teens dying each day.**

It you rewrote sentence 4 beginning

Unfortunately, about eleven teens die each day

the next word should be

(1) driving
(2) while
(3) drunk
(4) because
(5) although

12. Sentence 5: **It is clear that drunk driving is a serious problem in the United States, however, how to solve the problem is not as obvious.**

What correction should be made to this sentence?

(1) replace It is with Its
(2) insert a comma after that
(3) change the spelling of United to Unitted
(4) replace States, with States;
(5) remove the comma after however

13. Sentence 7: **Neither curfews nor educational programs is going to prevent all accidents, but it is hoped that, together, they will reduce the number due to alcohol.**

What correction should be made to this sentence?

(1) change the spelling of educational to educatianal
(2) change is going to are going
(3) replace accidents, but with accidents but,
(4) replace but it with but; it
(5) replace they will with they'll

14. Sentence 8: **Likewise, raising the licensing and drinking ages won't eliminate all car crashes, but such changes might cut down on accidents.**

What correction should be made to this sentence?

(1) Replace raising with rising
(2) Change the spelling of licensing to lisencing
(3) replace won't with wo'nt
(4) change the spelling of eliminate to elliminate
(5) no correction is necessary

15. Sentence 9: **After more studies have been done on the effectiveness of each method, it became more apparent which ones are the best.**

What correction should be made to this sentence?

(1) change have been to has been
(2) insert a comma after done
(3) replace method, it with method. It
(4) change became to will become
(5) change the spelling of apparent to aparrent

16. Sentences 10 & 11: **Then perhaps we can find a more consistent way to fight the nation's number one killer of teenagers. That killer is drunk driving accidents.**

The most effective combination of sentences 10 and 11 would include which of the following groups of words?

(1) teenagers, that killer is drunk driving accidents.
(2) teenagers, and that killer is drunk driving accidents.
(3) teenagers, whose killer is drunk driving accidents.
(4) teenagers; that killer is drunk driving accidents.
(5) teenagers, drunk driving accidents.

Items 17 to 23 are based on the following paragraph.

(1) The nation's highway rest areas are used by thousands of people each year. (2) With their bathrooms and restaurants, weary travelers usually find these areas a welcome sight. (3) Something new has been added to many of the larger rest areas. (4) Now they often have a computer for use in finding out about recreational offerings throughout the state. (5) A typical program displays a numbered list of activities on a screen. (6) The list might include trips to museums, skiing, and amusement parks. (7) Suppose that you stop at a rest area in New Haven, Connecticut and find such a computer their. (8) If you want to find out about nearby museums you should look for the number next to "museums" on the screen. (9) Press it, and instantly on the screen appears a map of Connecticut with numbered regions. (10) Find the number for New Haven, type it on the keyboard, and you will see a list of museums located in the vicinity. (11) After reading the entry for the Peabody Museum, you may decide to go and see the dinosaur exhibit there. (12) Although you undoubtedly could have found the same information without a computer, it would have taken more time and energy.

17. Sentence 2: **With their bathrooms and restaurants, weary travelers usually find these areas a welcome sight.**

Which of the following is the best way to write the underlined portion of this sentence? If you think the original is the best way, choose option (1).

(1) weary travelers usually find these areas a welcome sight.

(2) weary travelers usually found these areas a welcome sight.

(3) finding these areas is usually welcomed by weary travelers.

(4) these sights were usually welcomed by weary travelers.

(5) these areas are usually a welcome sight to weary travelers.

18. Sentence 4: **Now they often have a computer for use in finding out about recreational offerings throughout the state.**

What correction should be made to this sentence?

(1) replace they often have with it often has

(2) change have to had

(3) change the spelling of throughout to throuout

(4) change state to State

(5) no correction is necessary

19. Sentence 6: **The list might include trips to museums, skiing, and amusement parks.**

What correction should be made to this sentence?

(1) insert which after list

(2) change might include to included

(3) replace include trips with include; trips

(4) change museums to Museums

(5) replace skiing with ski resorts

20. Sentence 7: **Suppose that you stop at a rest area in New Haven, Connecticut, and find such a computer their.**

What correction should be made to this sentence?

(1) replace you stop with having stopped

(2) change New to new

(3) replace and with but

(4) change find to finding

(5) replace their with there

21. Sentence 8: **If you want to find out about nearby museums you should look for the number next to "museums" on the screen.**

What correction should be made to this sentence?

(1) replace <u>you want</u> with <u>one wants</u>
(2) insert a comma after <u>museums</u>
(3) replace <u>look for</u> with <u>look; for</u>
(4) replace <u>for</u> with <u>four</u>
(5) no correction is necessary

22. Sentence 9: **<u>Press it,</u> and instantly on the screen appears a map of Connecticut with numbered regions.**

Which of the following is the best way to write the underlined portion of this sentence? If you think the original is the best way, choose option (1).

(1) Press it,
(2) Pressing it,
(3) Press that number on the keyboard,
(4) Pressing that number on the keyboard.
(5) After pressing that number on the keyboard,

23. Sentence 12: **Although you undoubtedly could have found the same information without a computer, it would have taken more time and energy.**

If you rewrote sentence 12 beginning with

<u>Without a computer,</u>

the next word should be

(1) although
(2) you
(3) the
(4) it's
(5) time

Items 24 to 31 are based on the following paragraph.

(1) A group of editors has made a list of the fifty items that have changed our lives most in the past fifty years. (2) The editors work for Consumer Reports, a popular consumer magazine. (3) Not surprisingly, smoke detectors had been selected for the list. (4) After they were invented, a considerable number of lives were saved. (5) In many states, the law requires that they be installed in new houses. (6) Furthermore, many home insurance companies offer a discount to homeowners who use smoke detectors. (7) Smoke detectors operate on one of two principals, but both types produce a shrill noise to warn you of the presence of smoke. (8) One type detects smoke with light, the other type uses a minute amount of radiation. (9) Some people worry about its possible hazards, but it actually gives off less radiation than a television. (10) After making sure the detectors are installed according to the directions you need to clean them annually. (11) A special signal warning when the batteries are running down and need to be replaced. (12) With minimal maintenance, a smoke detector will wake sleepers which might not have become aware of a fire until too late.

24. Sentence 2: **The editors work for Consumer Reports, a popular consumer magazine.**

   What correction should be made to this sentence?

   (1) change editors to Editors
   (2) change Reports to reports
   (3) remove the comma after Reports
   (4) change consumer to Consumer
   (5) no correction is necessary

25. Sentence 3: **Not surprisingly, smoke detectors had been selected for the list.**

   Which of the following is the best way to write the underlined portion of this sentence? If you think the original is the best way, choose option (1).

   (1) detectors had been selected
   (2) detectors have been selected
   (3) detectors which had been selected
   (4) detectors has been selected
   (5) detectors are selected

26. Sentence 7: **Smoke detectors operate on one of two principals, but both types produce a shrill noise to warn you of the presence of smoke.**

   What correction should be made to this sentence?

   (1) change operate to operates
   (2) change the spelling of principals to principles
   (3) remove the comma after principals
   (4) replace but with for
   (5) change produce to producing

27. Sentence 8: **One type detects smoke with light, the other type uses a minute amount of radiation.**

   Which of the following is the best way to write the underlined portion of this sentence? If you think the original is the best way, choose option (1).

   (1) light, the other type uses
   (2) light; the other type uses
   (3) light; and the other type uses
   (4) light the other type uses
   (5) light; the other type using

28. Sentence 9: **Some people worry about its possible hazards, but it actually gives off less radiation than a television.**

What correction should be made to this sentence?

(1) change <u>worry</u> to <u>worries</u>
(2) replace <u>its</u> with <u>it's</u>
(3) replace <u>its possible hazards</u> with <u>the possible hazards of the latter</u>
(4) replace <u>than</u> with <u>then</u>
(5) no correction is necessary

29. Sentence 10: **After making sure the detectors are installed according to the directions you need to clean them annually.**

What correction should be made to this sentence?

(1) change <u>are</u> to <u>having been</u>
(2) change the spelling of <u>directions</u> to <u>derections</u>
(3) insert a comma after <u>directions</u>
(4) replace <u>you need</u> with <u>one needs</u>
(5) change the spelling of <u>annually</u> to <u>annaully</u>

30. Sentence 11: **A special <u>signal warning when the batteries are running down</u> and need to be replaced.**

Which of the following is the best way to write the underlined portion of this sentence? If you think the original is the best way, choose option (1).

(1) signal warning when the batteries are running down
(2) signal warns when the batteries are running down
(3) signal warned when the batteries are running down
(4) signal warning when the batteries is running down
(5) signal warning when the batteries have ran down

31. Sentence 12: **With minimal maintenance, a smoke detector will wake sleepers which might not have become aware of a fire until too late.**

What correction should be made to this sentence?

(1) change the spelling of <u>maintenance</u> to <u>maintenence</u>
(2) change <u>wake</u> to <u>woke</u>
(3) replace <u>which</u> with <u>who</u>
(4) replace <u>which</u> with <u>whom</u>
(5) replace <u>too</u> with <u>to</u>

Items 32 to 39 are based on the following paragraph.

(1) One thing that appears frequently in today's news is U.S. immigration laws. (2) For many years, there are disagreements about whom to allow entry and citizenship. (3) In 1790, Congress passed a ruling. (4) One had to live in the U.S. for two years, and then one could become a citizen. (5) In 1882, laws were passed, they were to keep out Chinese immigrants. (6) The Californian workers, more than anyone else, favored the laws because they wanted to reduce job competition. (7) In 1920, a quota system was established, specifying how many people could enter the U.S. anually from each foreign country. (8) Then in 1965, the quota system was replaced, by one giving preference to specialists, refugees, and citizens' relatives. (9) From Mexico come many illegal immigrants who are currently the center of a great deal of controversy. (10) Some senators and representatives in congress think that employers who hire illegal immigrants should be heavily fined. (11) Others, like senator Edward Kennedy, fear that such fines will lead to discrimination, especially against Hispanics. (12) It is not easy to find a solution that protects the rights of both those who are now citizens yet those who would like to be.

32. Sentence 1: **One thing that appears frequently in today's news is U.S. immigration laws.**

    If you rewrote sentence 1 beginning with

    U.S. immigration laws

    the next word should be

    (1) which
    (2) appear
    (3) that
    (4) being
    (5) were

33. Sentence 2: **For many years, there are disagreements about whom to allow entry and citizenship.**

    Which of the following is the best way to write the underlined portion of this sentence? If you think the original is the best way, choose option (1).

    (1) there are disagreements about whom to allow
    (2) there have been disagreements about whom to allow
    (3) there has been disagreements about whom to allow
    (4) there are disagreements, about whom to allow
    (5) there are disagreements about who to allow

34. Sentences 3 & 4: **In 1790, Congress passed a ruling. One had to live in the U.S. for two years, and then one could become a citizen.**

    The most effective combination of sentences 3 and 4 would include which of the following groups of words?

    (1) Congress had to live
    (2) ruling, and one had
    (3) that anyone who had lived
    (4) ruling, anyone could live
    (5) ruling, and after becoming

35. Sentence 5: **In 1882, <u>laws were passed, they were to keep out</u> Chinese immigrants.**

    Which of the following is the best way to write the underlined portion of this sentence? If you think the original is the best way, choose option (1).

    (1) laws were passed, they were to keep out
    (2) laws were passed, and they were to keep out
    (3) laws were passed. Keeping out
    (4) laws were passed, because of keeping out
    (5) laws were passed to keep out

36. Sentence 8: **Then in 1965, the quota system <u>was replaced, by one giving preference to specialists, refugees,</u> and citizens' relatives.**

    Which of the following is the best way to write the underlined portion of this sentence? If you think the original is the best way, choose option (1).

    (1) was replaced, by one giving preference to specialists, refugees,
    (2) is replaced, by one giving preference to specialists, refugees,
    (3) was replaced by one giving preference to specialists, refugees,
    (4) was replaced. One giving preference to specialists, refugees,
    (5) was replaced, by one giving preference to specialists refugees.

37. Sentence 10: **Some senators and representatives in congress think that employers who hire illegal immigrants should be heavily fined.**

    What correction should be made to this sentence?

    (1) change <u>senators</u> to <u>Senators</u>
    (2) change <u>congress</u> to <u>Congress</u>
    (3) change <u>think</u> to <u>thinks</u>
    (4) replace <u>who</u> with <u>that</u>
    (5) no correction is necessary

38. Sentence 11: **Others, like senator Edward Kennedy, fear that such fines will lead to discrimination, especially against Hispanics.**

    What correction should be made to this sentence?

    (1) change *senator* to *Senator*
    (2) remove the comma after *Kennedy*
    (3) change *fear* to *fears*
    (4) change the spelling of *discrimination* to *disscrimination*
    (5) no correction is necessary

39. Sentence 12: **It is not easy to find a solution that protects the rights of both those who are now citizens yet those who would like to be.**

    What correction should be made to this sentence?

    (1) replace <u>is not</u> with <u>not being</u>
    (2) insert a comma after <u>solution</u>
    (3) replace <u>who</u> with <u>which</u>
    (4) replace <u>citizens, yet</u> with <u>citizens; yet</u>
    (5) replace <u>yet</u> with <u>and</u>

Items 40 to 47 are based on the following paragraph.

(1) There is many ways you can help a child improve his or her writing skills. (2) During an ordinary day, there are often times when even young children can help you with writing tasks. (3) Before going to the supermarket or hardware store for example, you could ask the child to help you make a list. (4) Older children can be showed how to take accurate telephone messages. (5) Rather than buying Valentine's Day or other Holiday cards, you can suggest that children make cards and add their own messages. (6) After you do something interesting with a child, such as go to a ballgame or visiting an aquarium, suggest writing to someone about it. (7) If you live at a distance from a young cousin, niece, nephew, or grandchild, you could write to the child. (8) By asking a few simple questions in your letter, you will encourage the child to write back. (9) Perhaps the most powerful means of encouraging children to write are by acting as a good role model. (10) A child might see you writing frequently. (11) If the child respects you, he or she will believe that you are earnest about the value of this activity.

40. Sentence 1: **There is many ways you can help a child improve his or her writing skills.**

Which of the following is the best way to write the underlined portion of this sentence? If you think the original is the best way, choose option (1).

(1) There is many ways you can help a child
(2) There are many ways you can help a child
(3) There being many ways you can help a child
(4) There is many ways one can help a child
(5) There is many ways, you can help a child

41. Sentence 3: **Before going to the supermarket or hardware store for example, you could ask the child to help you make a list.**

What correction should be made to this sentence?

(1) change supermarket to Supermarket
(2) insert a comma after store
(3) remove the comma after example
(4) replace you could with one could
(5) change make to making

42. Sentence 4: **Older children can be showed how to take accurate telephone messages.**

Which of the following is the best way to write the underlined portion of this sentence? If you think the original is the best way, choose option (1).

(1) Older children can be showed how to take
(2) Older children, can be showed how to take
(3) Older children could be showed how to take
(4) Older children can be shown how to take
(5) Older children can be showed how are taken

43. Sentence 5: **Rather than buying Valentine's Day or other Holiday cards, you can suggest that children make cards and add their own messages.**

What correction should be made to this sentence?

(1) change Valentine's Day to valentine's day
(2) insert a comma after Day
(3) change Holiday to holiday
(4) change add to added
(5) replace their with there

44. Sentence 6: **After you do something interesting with a child, <u>such as go to a ballgame or visiting an aquarium, suggest</u> writing to someone about it.**

Which of the following is the best way to write the underlined portion of this sentence? If you think the original is the best way, choose option (1).

(1) such as go to a ballgame or visiting an aquarium, suggest

(2) such as going to a ballgame or visiting an aquarium, suggest

(3) such as go to a ballgame, or visiting an aquarium, suggest

(4) such as go to a ballgame or visiting an Aquarium, suggest

(5) such as go to a ballgame or visiting an aquarium. Suggest

45. Sentence 8: **By asking a few simple questions in your letter, you will encourage the child to write back.**

What correction should be made to this sentence?

(1) replace <u>your</u> with <u>you're</u>

(2) remove the comma after <u>letter</u>

(3) replace <u>you will</u> with <u>one will</u>

(4) replace <u>you will encourage the child</u> with <u>the child will want</u>

(5) no correction is necessary

46. Sentence 9: **Perhaps the most powerful means of encouraging children to write are by acting as a good role model.**

What correction should be made to this sentence?

(1) change the spelling of <u>encouraging</u> to <u>encouragging</u>

(2) insert a comma after <u>write</u>

(3) change <u>are</u> to <u>is</u>

(4) replace <u>role</u> with <u>roll</u>

(5) no correction is necessary

47. Sentences 10 & 11: **A child might see you writing frequently. If the child respects you, he or she will believe that you are earnest about the value of this activity.**

The most effective combination of sentences 10 and 11 would include which of the following groups of words?

(1) If a child who respects you sees you writing

(2) If he or she respects you and sees you writing

(3) A child might see you writing frequently, and if

(4) they will believe that you are earnest about

(5) then children will share one's earnest respect

Items 48 to 55 are based on the following paragraphs.

(1) In the late 1800s, music was a popular pasttime. (2) Wealthy people attended the opera and the symphony. (3) Many more people had gone to vaudeville shows or listened to ragtime music. (4) Vaudeville was a variety show that included comedy acts, song-and-dance routines, and performers involved in acrobatics. (5) Ragtime was a new rhythmic music with a lively sound. (6) Scott Joplin, son of a freed slave, helped make ragtime popular. (7) His "Maple Leaf Rag," written in 1899, was a nationwide hit.

(8) American songwriters produced many popular songs. (9) Even though the radio had not yet been invented, songs such as "There'll Be a Hot Time in the Old Town Tonight" swept the nation in weeks. (10) New songs were played in music halls and on vaudville stages. (11) Among the most popular was military marches written by John Philip Sousa. (12) Sousa has written more than 100 marches, including "The Stars and Stripes Forever." (13) His marches became favorites at Fourth of July celebrations.

48. Sentence 1: **In the late 1800s, music was a popular pasttime.**

    What correction should be made to this sentence?

    (1) change pasttime to pastime
    (2) remove the comma after 1800s
    (3) insert an apostrophe before the s in 1800s
    (4) change was to had been
    (5) no correction is necessary

49. Sentence 3: **Many more people had gone to vaudeville shows or listened to ragtime music.**

    What correction should be made to this sentence?

    (1) insert a comma after shows
    (2) insert had after or
    (3) insert a comma after gone
    (4) change had gone to went
    (5) no correction is necessary

50. Sentence 4: **Vaudeville was a variety show that included comedy acts, song-and-dance routines, and performers involved in acrobatics.**

    Which of the following is the best way to write the underlined portion of this sentence? If you think the original is the best way, choose option (1).

    (1) included comedy acts, song-and-dance routines, and performers involved in acrobatics
    (2) including comedy acts, singers, dancers, and performers involved in acrobatics
    (3) included comedy acts, song-and-dance routines, and acrobatics
    (4) included comedy acts, song-and-dance routines, and, acrobats
    (5) included comedy acts, song-and-dance routines, and, acrobatics

51. Sentence 5: **Ragtime was a new rhythmic music with a lively sound.**

    What correction should be made to this sentence?

    (1) change <u>was</u> to <u>is</u>
    (2) change the spelling of <u>rhythmic</u> to <u>rythmic</u>
    (3) insert a comma after <u>rhythmic</u>
    (4) insert a comma after <u>new</u>
    (5) no correction is necessary

52. Sentence 7: **His "Maple Leaf Rag," written in 1899, was a nationwide hit.**

    What correction should be made to this sentence?

    (1) remove the comma after <u>Rag</u>
    (2) remove the comma after <u>1899</u>
    (3) change <u>"Maple Leaf Rag"</u> to <u>"Maple leaf rag"</u>
    (4) change <u>"Maple Leaf Rag"</u> to <u>"maple leaf rag"</u>
    (5) no correction is necessary

53. Sentence 9: **Even though the radio had not yet been invented, songs such as "There'll Be a Hot Time in the Old Town Tonight" swept the nation in weeks.**

    If you rewrote sentence 9 beginning with

    <u>Songs such as "There'll Be a Hot Time in the Old Town Tonight"</u>

    the next words should be

    (1) sweeped the nation in weeks because
    (2) swept the nation in weeks since
    (3) swept the nation in weeks but
    (4) swept the nation in weeks, however,
    (5) swept the nation in weeks although

54. Sentence 11: **Among the most <u>popular was military marches written by</u> John Philip Sousa.**

    Which of the following is the best way to write the underlined portion of this sentence? If you think the original is the best way, choose option (1).

    (1) popular was military marches written by
    (2) popular were military marches written by
    (3) popular is military marches written by
    (4) popular are military marches written by
    (5) popular were military marches written by,

55. Sentence 12: **Sousa <u>has written more than 100 marches, including</u> "The Stars and Stripes Forever."**

    Which of the following is the best way to write the underlined portion of this sentence? If you think the original is the best way, choose option (1).

    (1) has written more than 100 marches, including
    (2) has wrote more than 100 marches, including
    (3) has written more than 100 marches including
    (4) wrote more than 100 marches, including,
    (5) wrote more than 100 marches, including

Check your answers. Correct answers are on pages 92–95.

Simulated Test
Part II

TIME: 45 minutes

DIRECTIONS: This is a test to see how well you can write. In this test, you are asked to write an essay in which you present your opinions about an issue. In preparing your essay, you should take the following steps.

Step 1. Read all of the information about the topic. Be sure that you understand the topic and that you write about only the assigned topic.

Step 2. Plan your essay before you write.

Step 3. Use scrap paper to make any notes.

Step 4. Write your essay on a separate sheet of paper.

Step 5. Read what you have written. Make sure that your writing is legible.

Step 6. Check your paragraphing, sentence structure, spelling, punctuation, capitalization, and usage; make any changes that will improve your essay.

TOPIC

Radio was once the most important medium of communication in the world. It was also one of the most popular forms of entertainment for a period of about 25 years. It has been replaced, in both respects, by television.

Write an essay of 200 words in which you state whether you prefer one medium of communication rather than the other. Compare the use of radio and television as sources of information, entertainment, or both. Be specific, and use examples to support your point of view.

When you take the GED test, you will have 45 minutes to write about the topic question you are assigned. Try to write the essay for this unit test within 45 minutes. Write legibly and use a ballpoint pen so that your writing will be easy to read. Any notes that you make on scrap paper will not be counted as part of your score.

After you complete this essay use the Essay Scoring Guide and Model Essays in the answer key to score your essay. They will be concerned with how clearly you make the main point of your essay, how thoroughly you support your ideas, and how clear and correct your writing is throughout the composition. You will receive no credit for writing about a question other than the one assigned.

Answers are on pages 97–98.

Performance Analysis Chart
Part I

Directions: Circle the number of each item that you got correct on the Simulated Test. Count how many items you got correct in each row; count how many items you got correct in each column. Write the amount correct per row and column as the numerator in the fraction in the appropriate "Total Correct" box. (The denominators represent the total number of items in the row or column.) Write the grand total correct over the denominator **55** at the lower right corner of the chart. (For example, if you got 50 items correct, write *50* so that the fraction reads 50/**55**.)

Item Type	Usage (Chapter 1)	Sentence Structure (Chapter 2)	Mechanics (Chapter 3)	TOTAL CORRECT
Construction Shift	2, 32	11, 16, 23, 34, 47, 53		/8
Sentence Correction	5, 10, 13, 15, 18, 28, 31, 46, 49	4, 12, 19, 39, 45	8, 9, 14, 20, 21, 24, 26, 29, 37, 38, 41, 43, 48, 51, 52	/29
Sentence Revision	3, 22, 25, 33, 40, 42, 54, 55	1, 6, 17, 27, 30, 35, 44, 50	7, 36	/18
TOTAL CORRECT	/19	/19	/17	/55

The Unit I chapters named in parentheses indicate where in the Writing Skills instruction of the *New Revised Cambridge GED Program: Comprehensive Book* you can find specific instruction about the areas of grammar you encountered on the Simulated Test. You can find more in-depth instruction in the *New Revised Cambridge GED Program: Writing Skills*.

On the chart, items are classified as Construction Shift, Sentence Correction, and Sentence Revision. These three item types are introduced in the *New Revised Cambridge GED Program: Comprehensive Book* and the *New Revised Cambridge GED Program: Writing Skills*.

Part II

Directions: After you have used the guidelines in the Answers and Explanations section of this book to score your essay, make a record of your evaluation here:

Write the score of your essay in the box at the right.

List some of the strong points of your essay.

List some of the weak points of your essay.

List improvements that you plan to make when you work on your next essay

Answers and Explanations

Chapter 1 Usage
Skill 1 Subject-Verb Agreement

Lesson 1

1. ***Everybody helps*** to *clean up the house on Saturday mornings.* Change *help* to *helps* to agree with *everybody* which is a singular subject.
2. *The committee* ***members were*** *discussing the issue before the vote.* Change *was* to *were* to agree with *members.*
3. Correct. *Were* agrees with the plural subject *concerts.*
4. *Many* ***children enjoy*** *building sand castles at the beach.* Change *enjoys* to *enjoy* to agree with *children.*
5. *Few* ***meteors were*** *sighted during the sky-watch.* Change *was* to *were* to agree with *meteors.*
6. *The personnel* ***director posts*** *the list of job openings once a month.* Change *post* to *posts* to agree with *director.*
7. Correct. *Were* agrees with *systems.*
8. ***No one has*** *failed to notice the new maple trees in the park.* Change *have* to *has* to agree with *no one.*
9. *The* ***jury is prepared*** *to announce its verdict.* Change *are* to *is* to agree with *jury,* which in this case is singular since it describes individuals working together as a unit.
10. *Many* ***houses benefit*** *from additional insulation.* Change *benefits* to *benefit* to agree with *houses.*

Lesson 2

1. *The shortest* ***distance*** *between two points* ***is*** *a straight line.* Change *are* to *is* to agree with the singular subject *distance.*
2. *Several* ***proposals*** *for a mass transit system* ***include*** *the construction of a monorail.* Change *includes* to *include* to agree with plural subject *proposals.*
3. *The asparagus* ***plant,*** *along with several varieties of beans,* ***grows*** *easily in this soil.* Change *grow* to *grows* to agree with singular subject *plant.*

4. Correct. *One* agrees with *was.*
5. ***Accuracy*** *in design and production* ***has*** *earned a good reputation for that tool company.* Change *have* to *has* to agree with singular subject *accuracy.*
6. ***Tea,*** *as well as coffee and many soft drinks,* ***contains*** *caffeine.* Change *contain* to *contains* to agree with singular subject *tea.*
7. ***Physics,*** *as well as chemistry,* ***is*** *a required course for third-year students.* Change *are* to *is* to agree with singular subject *physics.*
8. *The* ***location*** *of a house* ***is*** *one factor affecting the selling price.* Change *are* to *is* to agree with singular subject *location.*
9. Correct. *Terriers* agrees with *are.*
10. ***One*** *of Robert Frost's most famous poems* ***is*** *"Birches."* Change *are* to *is* to agree with singular subject *one.*

Lesson 3

1. *At the concert* ***were Jane and her brothers.*** In subject—verb order, this sentence reads: *Jane and her brothers were at the concert.* Change *was* to *were* to agree with *Jane and her brothers.*
2. ***Were*** *the* ***results*** *of the diving competition already announced?* In subject—verb order, this sentence reads: *The results of the diving competition were already announced.* Change *was* to *were* to agree with *results.*
3. Correct. This sentence does not have inverted structure. The verb *were* immediately follows the subject *employees.*
4. Correct. This sentence does not have inverted structure. The verb *enjoys* immediately follows the subject *Jerry.*
5. ***Is*** *the new communications* ***system*** *more efficient than the old one?* In subject—verb order, this sentence reads: *The new communications system is more efficient than the old one.* Change *are* to *is* to agree with singular subject *system.*
6. *On the lake* ***were a swan and several geese.*** In subject—verb order this sentence reads: *A swan and several geese were on the lake.* Change *was* to *were* to agree with *a swan and several geese.*

7. *Around the playground* **runs** *a high* **fence.** In subject—verb order, this sentence reads: *A high fence runs around the play- ground.* Change *run* to *runs* to agree with *fence.*

8. *On each side of the road* **were signs** *advertising restaurants.* In subject—verb order, this sentence reads: *Signs advertis- ing restaurants were on each side of the road.* Change *was* to *were* to agree with *signs.*

9. Correct. In subject—verb order, this sen- tence reads: *The hurricane was as dan- gerous as last year's storm. Was* agrees with *hurricane.*

10. **Is** *the* **quality** *of these shirts related to the price?* In subject—verb order, this sentence reads: *The quality of these shirts is related to the price.* Change *are* to *is* to agree with singular subject, *quality.*

Lesson 4

1. *Here* **are** *the most recent* **issues** *of that magazine.* Subject—*issues;* verb—*are.*

2. Correct. Subject—*site;* verb—*was.*

3. *There* **were** *approximately one million* **inhabitants** *of the city of Rome in ancient times.* Plural subject—*inhabitants;* verb— *were.*

4. Correct. Subject—*house;* verb—*is.*

5. *There* **are** *six* **states** *in the New England region.* Subject—*states;* verb—*are.*

6. *Here* **is** *the* **money** *I owe you for lunch last week.* Singular subject—*money;* verb—*is.*

7. *There* **are** *about 40 million* **Americans** *affected by diabetes and its related dis- eases.* Subject—*Americans;* verb—*are.*

8. *Here* **are** *the new* **radio and earphones** *you ordered.* Subjects—*radio and ear- phones;* verb—*are.*

9. *There* **are** *1500* **languages and dialects** *spoken in India.* Subjects—*languages and dialects;* verb—*are.*

10. *There* **are** *three television* **debates** *sched- uled between the candidates.* Subject— *debates;* verb—*are.*

Lesson 5

1. *Both* **a keyboard and a monitor are** *basic parts of a computer system.* Two subjects joined by *both...and* require a plural verb.

2. *Either Irma or* **her sister** *is planning to compete in the race.* Since the subjects are joined by either...or and the closer subject, *sister* is singular, a singular verb is required.

3. Correct. The plural verb **make** agrees in number with the plural subject that is nearest to it—*flight attendants.*

4. *Neither the pay* **nor the working condi- tions were** *satisfactory in that office.* The verb must agree in number with the plur- al subject that is nearest to it when two subjects are joined by *neither...nor.*

5. *Either Rick* **or Phil has repaired** *the chairs.* Since the subjects are joined by *either...or* and the closer subject, *Phil,* is singular, the verb must be singular.

6. Correct. Subjects joined by *and* require a plural verb.

7. *Neither the governor nor the lieutenant governor* **has signed** *this bill into law.* Since the subjects are joined by *nei- ther...nor* and the closer subject, *governor,* is singular, the verb must be singular.

8. Correct. Subjects joined by *and* require a plural verb.

9. *Not only the town's mayor* **but also the chief** *of police* **is** *African American.* Since the subjects are joined by *not only...but also* and the closer subject, *chief,* is sin- gular the verb must be singular.

10. *Either the doctor or the nurse* **gives** *the injections.* Since both subjects are joined by *either...or* and the closer subject, *nurse,* is singular, the verb must be sin- gular.

Skill 2 Verb Tense

Lesson 1

1. *Drunk drivers* **cause** *many fatal accidents each year on the nation's highways.*

2. *In ancient times, many people* **thought** *that omens predicted the future.*

3. *Last spring, the tulips* **grew** *very well in this soil.*

4. *Hank may have problems if he* **chooses** *to accept that job.*

5. *The average building on this block* **con- tains** *eight apartments.*

6. *Have you* **driven** *the car all the way to Indianapolis?*

7. *Martha has* **lain** *down for quite a while.*

8. *The geese always take flight several min- utes after the sun* **has risen.**

9. *Chuck admits that he* **has known** *about the job opening since he told Randy about it.*

10. *Are they aware of what they* **have done?**

Lesson 2

1. *The first modern income tax **was assessed** in England around 1800.* The date is a clue that the action should be expressed in the past tense.

2. *Next Saturday, the Rangers **will play** the Bruins. Next Saturday* is a clue that the future tense should be used.

3. *Do you think that Robert **will receive** his degree next year?* The words *next year* are a clue that the future tense should be used.

4. *The Civil War **took** place between 1861 and 1865.* Since the sentence is about a historical event, the past tense must be used.

5. *Today, many people **take** mass transportation to get to work.* The word *Today* is a clue that the present tense should be used to describe a general condition.

6. *Correct.* The words *on Sundays* are a clue that a general condition is being described.

7. *Last week, Helen **received** a perfect score on her geography test.* The words *Last week* are a clue that the past tense is required.

8. *The catalytic converter has **reduced** pollution from automobiles for the last 5 years.* The words *for the past 5 years* are a clue that the past tense is required.

9. *Correct. At the moment* is a clue that the present tense should be used.

10. *John **will meet** us later after the movie.* The word *later* is a clue that the future tense should be used.

Lesson 3

1. *An earthquake is a violent movement of the Earth's surface. Earthquakes sometimes **begin** with slight tremors and then **increase** in the intensity of the shock. The most common cause of earthquakes is a sudden stress along a fault line in the Earth's crust. This stress **leads** to vibrations that pass through the earth. A scale called the Richter scale measures the amount of energy released by a quake.* Because the paragraph describes the general characteristics of earthquakes, the present tense should be used.

2. *When we **visited** New York last year at Christmas, the city was magical. Many department stores **had** lovely window displays, and the streets **were** full of holiday shoppers. We visited Central Park, which glistened in the snow, and we **attended** several concerts. I especially **enjoyed** see-*

*ing the great tree at Rockefeller Center. Since our whole family **was** together for the first time in many months, the trip was a special treat.* Because the paragraph describes an event in the past, the past tense should be used throughout the paragraph.

Lesson 4

1. *Light bulbs were on sale yesterday, and Mrs. Polk **bought** a dozen.* The verb *buy* should be in the past tense to be consistent with the past tense verb *were*.

2. *When the gates open, cars **will be** able to proceed.* The second part of the sentence should be in the future tense since a cause-effect relationship is expressed.

3. *Forecasters predict that snow **will fall** later this week in the mountains.* The future tense should be used since the sentence concerns a prediction.

4. *When the runners finally came into the stretch, we **saw** that Marla was leading.* The verb should be in the past tense to be consistent with the past-tense verb *came* in the first part of the sentence.

5. *Sam thinks that the voters **will send** the mayor a message next November. Next November* provides a clue that the verb should be in the future tense.

6. *That deli is new, and the sandwiches **are** some of the best I have ever eaten.* The verb should be in the present tense to be consistent with the present-tense verb *is*.

7. *As the threats to world peace multiply, the price of gold generally **rises.*** Since a general condition is being described, both verbs should be in the present tense.

8. *Cats are popular pets, and they soon **will outnumber** dogs in American households.* The word *soon* provides a clue that the verb should be in the future tense.

9. *As clouds covered the sun, the temperature **fell.*** The verb should be in the past tense to be consistent with the past-tense verb *covered*.

10. *Few tall buildings are to be seen in that city, because earthquakes frequently **occur** there.* Since a general condition is being described, both verbs should be in the present tense.

Skill 3 Pronoun Reference

Lesson 1

1. *Some people like to record **their** thoughts every day in a diary.* Change *his* to *their* to agree with *people*.

2. *A governor **or a mayor** must be attentive to the needs of **his** [or **her**] constituents.* Change *their* to *his* [or *her*] to agree with the closer singular antecedent *governor*.

3. *The United States and Canada sent **their** leaders to the economic conference.* Change *its* to *their* to agree with the antecedents *United States* and *Canada*, which are joined by *and*.

4. Correct. *Their* and *them*, both of which are plural, refer to *members*.

5. *Marv and Jim were proud of **their** team's new record.* Change *his* to *their* to agree with *Marv and Jim*.

6. *The commuters boarded **their** bus at 7:30 A.M.* Change *his* to *their* to agree with *commuters*.

7. *The neighbors kindly invited us to **their** party.* Change *our* to *their* to agree with *neighbors*.

8. *Slipping on the ice, Mrs. Pennington fell and bruised **her** knee.* Change *its* to *her* to agree with *Mrs. Pennington*.

9. *To succeed, a newspaper **or a magazine** must appeal to **its** readers.* Change *their* to *its* to refer to the singular antecedent *magazine*.

10. Correct. *His* and *he* are singular, referring to the singular antecedent *president*.

Lesson 2

1. *When you interview for a job, **you** should remember to be courteous.*

2. *You should not eat so much cheese if **you** are trying to lose weight.*

3. *Ambitious people will always aim for perfection in everything **they** do.*

4. *When you buy an appliance, **you** should always save your receipt.*

5. Correct.

6. *On the first day of your new job, try to learn all **you** can about your responsibilities.*

7. *If we have any vacation time this summer, **we** will visit our relatives in Nebraska.*

8. *When you see that movie, you will be on the edge of **your** seat!*

9. *Exercise can relieve one's mental stress as well as improve his/her physical condition.* Since "one's" is third person singular, you must use either *his or her*.

10. Correct.

Lesson 3

1. *In English class, the writer **whom** I enjoyed most was Edgar Allan Poe.* Think of the pronoun *him* to arrive at the correct relative pronoun *whom*: I enjoyed *him* most.

2. *The Canadian goose is a bird **that** migrates to our area in the winter. That* or *which* refers to an animal or thing. **What** is not a relative pronoun.

3. Correct. Use *whom* to refer to people. The verb "admire" has a subject "I".

4. *Visitors to Washington **who** see the Lincoln Memorial seldom fail to be impressed. Who* refers to *people*.

5. *The flowers **that** I planted in the early spring have all bloomed. That* refers to things. *What* is not a relative pronoun.

6. *The article **that** I read predicted a sharp increase in car sales. What* is not a relative pronoun. *That* refers to a thing (article).

7. *Shoppers **who** present this coupon are eligible for a discount.* **Whom** is used as the relative pronoun when the noun referred to is an object (as in "shoppers to **whom** coupons are given are eligible for a discount.") **Who** is used when the noun to which it refers is a subject, as in sentence #7. **Who** and **whom** are the relative pronouns that refer to people.

8. Correct. *Which* refers to the city of *St. Paul*.

9. Correct. *Who* refers to *Ponce de Leon*.

10. *The cardinal, **which** is a member of the finch family, has a crest and a red bill. Which* is the relative pronoun used to refer to animals.

Lesson 4

The rewording of some sentences may vary from the examples shown below.

1. *Clara is not in the office this week because she is on vacation.* Reword the sentence to eliminate *which; which* has no clear antecedent.

2. *Jenna wants to be a salesperson because salespeople earn good commissions.* Substitute *salespeople* for *they; they* has no clear antecedent.

3. *The governor, whom the majority of the state's voters support, has spoken in favor of that proposal.* The phrase beginning with *whom* should be moved, as shown, so that the antecedent of *whom* is clear.

4. *A newspaper I read published an interesting article about Alaska.* Reword the sentence to eliminate *they; they* has no clear antecedent. Or: *In a newspaper I read, a reporter wrote an interesting article about Alaska.*

5. Correct. *Which* has a clear antecedent, *fare.*

6. *The lines to get into the museum are so long because this exhibit is very popular.* Reword the sentence to eliminate *which; which* has no clear antecedent.

7. *John wants to study for a career in medicine because doctors are dedicated to helping people.* Substitute *doctors* for *they; they* has no clear antecedent.

8. *Although the fire broke out at 10:00 P.M., the fire department did not reach the house until fifteen minutes later.* Substitute a noun for the pronoun *they.*

9. *The fishing expedition was canceled because the meteorologists predicted high winds on the lake.* Reword the sentence to eliminate *which; which* has no clear antecedent.

10. *John and his sister want to study engineering because engineers will be in demand in the coming decades.* Substitute a noun for the pronoun *they.*

Lesson 5

The rewording of some sentences may vary from the examples given below.

1. *Because of the mayor's new proposal,* **he and the treasurer** *were criticized in today's editorial.* OR *Because of the treasurer's new proposal,* **he and the mayor** *were criticized in today's editorial.* Reword the sentence so that *he* clearly refers to one person—either the mayor or the treasurer.

2. *The director told the actor that* **he, the director** *needed a new approach.* OR *The director told the actor that* **he, the actor,** *needed a new approach.* Reword the sentence so that he clearly refers to one person—either the director or the actor.

3. *One of my nephews told my father that* **he, my nephew,** *would get a raise.* OR *One of my nephews told my father that* **he, my father,** *would get a raise.* Reword the sentence so that *he* clearly refers to one person—either the nephew or the father.

4. *The most famous novel of Cervantes is* **Don Quixote,** *who is a romantic adventurer.* OR

The most famous novel of the romantic adventurer **Cervantes** *is* Don Quixote. Eliminate the ambiguous pronoun *he,* which might refer to either Cervantes or Don Quixote.

5. *The librarian reminded Paul that* **he, the librarian,** *had already read that book.* OR *The librarian reminded Paul that* **he, Paul,** *had already read that book.* Reword the sentence so that *he* clearly refers to one person—either the librarian or Paul.

6. *The directors told the shareholders that* **they, the directors,** *could not expect the company to make a profit this year.* OR *The directors told the shareholders that* **they, the shareholders,** *could not expect the company to make a profit this year.* Reword the sentence so that *they* clearly refers to one group—either the directors or the shareholders.

7. *One of Mark Twain's very colorful* **novels** *is about life on the Mississippi.* OR *One of Mark Twain's novels is about the very colorful* **life on the Mississippi.** Eliminate the ambiguous pronoun *it,* which could refer to either the novel or to life on the Mississippi.

8. *Our cousins told the neighbors that the taxes* **our cousins** *paid were too high.* OR *Our cousins told the neighbors that the taxes* **the neighbors** *paid were too high.* Eliminate the ambiguous pronoun *they,* which could refer to either the cousins or the neighbors.

9. *This magazine carries many fascinating* **articles** *about exotic animals.* OR *This magazine carries many articles about fascinating, exotic* **animals.** Eliminate the ambiguous pronoun *they,* which could refer to either the articles or the animals.

10. *Our friends told the bus drivers that* **they, our friends,** *were going to be late.* OR *Our friends told the bus drivers that* **they, the bus drivers,** *were going to be late.* Reword the sentence so that *they* clearly refers to one group—the friends or the bus drivers.

Chapter 2   Sentence Structure
Skill 1 Complete Sentences

Lesson 1

There may be more than one correct way to edit some sentences.

1. *The Mississippi River* **is** *the longest river in North America.* Add a verb.

2. **The jury** reached a verdict after three hours. Add a subject.

3. **A good night's sleep is** the reward for a hard day's work. Add a subject and verb to complete the meaning.

4. *Although several inches of snow fell during the night,* **the roads were plowed by morning.** Add words to complete the meaning or omit "although."

5. **Most of the runners** found the ten-mile race exhausting. Add a subject.

6. Correct. This is a complete sentence.

7. *The term "canoe"* **refers** *to several types of thin, long boats.* Make *referring* the main verb by changing its form.

8. *Canada* **is** *the largest country in the Western Hemisphere.* Add a verb.

9. Correct. This is a complete sentence.

10. *Early people* **created** *art on the walls of caves.* Make *creating* the main verb by changing its form.

Lesson 2

The order of some sentences may vary from the examples shown below.

1. *The Rose Bowl is one of the country's largest stadiums. It is located in California.*

2. *The chipmunk is a kind of squirrel. There are more than 300 kinds of squirrels.*

3. *Mississippi's first newspaper was published in 1799. Today 25 daily newspapers are published in that state.*

4. *Spiders do not have teeth. They eat only liquids.*

5. *The stagecoach was used to transport passengers and mail. Sometimes it also carried freight.*

6. *Shirley Chisholm was the first black woman to serve in the U.S. Congress. She was elected in 1968.*

7. *The sponge was once considered a plant. It is actually an animal.*

8. *Philadelphia is the largest city in Pennsylvania. It is the fourth largest city in the country.*

9. Correct.

10. *The sport of paddle tennis was invented in 1898. City championships were first held in New York City in 1922.*

Lesson 3

There may be more than one correct way to edit some sentences.

1. *The zoo in Philadelphia opened in 1874; it is the oldest zoo in the country.*

2. *Butter has been used throughout history for many unusual purposes; for example, ancient Romans used it as a skin cream.*

3. *The development of a pearl within an oyster is a slow process; in fact, it may take three years for an oyster to produce a valuable pearl.*

4. Correct. This is not a run-on sentence.

5. *Red-winged blackbirds live in marshes, and they build their nests in the rushes.*

6. *Plants are the source of all our food; therefore, the study of plants is important.* OR *Plants are the source of all our food, so the study of plants is important.*

7. *The construction was not completed on schedule; as a result, the client withheld payment.* OR *The construction was not completed on schedule, so the client withheld payment.*

8. *Herbs are widely used in cooking. Many herbs are native to the Mediterranean countries.* Separate sentences are appropriate because the two ideas are not closely related.

9. *Musk turtles eat anything, but they prefer to eat animal food.*

10. *The southern states cover only about one-seventh of the country; however, nearly one-quarter of the American people live in the region.*

Skill 2 Coordination and Subordination

Lesson 1

1. *The influence of refrigerated railroad cars was great; for example, fresh food could travel vast distances without spoiling.* Use a coordinator that shows an example or reason.

2. Correct. *However* shows contrast.

3. *Many people registered to vote,* **for** *the upcoming election is an important one.* The second sentence gives the reason, not the result; therefore, use "for."

4. *Some kinds of pelicans can fly for hours. The pelican is one of the largest birds with webbed feet.* Divide these ideas into two sentences because they are not closely related.

5. Correct. *On the other hand* shows contrast.

6. *Fresh-water aquariums are inexpensive and easily maintained; consequently, many people enjoy owning them.* Use a coordinator that shows a conclusion.

7. *Ragweed grows quickly and is not easily noticed; hence, efforts to eliminate it have failed.* Use a coordinator that shows a conclusion.

8. *Quilting parties were common in the American colonies, and quilting is still a popular hobby. And* adds a related idea.

9. *The Grand Canyon was formed by glaciers and rushing water. Hundreds of tourists admire the sight each year.* Divide these two ideas into two sentences because they are not closely related.

10. *The Industrial Revolution began in Britain, and Britain has produced many important inventions. And* combines two related ideas about the Industrial Revolution in England.

Lesson 2

1. *Because democracy requires the participation of all citizens, it is important to vote.* When using a subordinator (*because*), do not use a coordinator (*then*).

2. *Until the advent of films with sound, a movie actor's voice was of no importance.* Use only one subordinator.

3. *Although letters are usually appreciated, they are rarely written.* Use a comma after a subordinate idea that comes first in the sentence.

4. *Some large lakes are called seas, although a lake is usually a fairly small body of water surrounded by land.* OR *While some lakes are called seas, a lake is usually a fairly small body of water surrounded by land.* Make one or the other clause in a sentence subordinate; do not make both clauses subordinate.

5. *While the library is open, you can listen to records or tapes.* Retain the second half of the sentence preceded by a comma. Use either *while* or *when*—not *even though,* which is used for contrasting ideas.

6. Correct.

7. *Unless it is cooked, eggplant is not pleasant to eat.* Use a comma after a subordinate idea that comes first in the sentence.

8. *As long as the clothing industry is an international business, people in many countries will dress similarly.* When using a subordinator (*as long as*), do not also use a coordinator (*so*).

9. Correct.

10. *Whenever he was invited to speak, Wilson gladly gave his opinion.* When using a subordinator (*whenever*), do not use a coordinator (*thus*).

In each of the following sentences, two sentences were combined to avoid repetitious words or phrases.

Lesson 3

There may be more than one correct way to edit some sentences.

1. *Ralph lent Maureen a fishing rod and a reel.*

2. *The letter and the telephone call concerned Ruth's tax return.*

3. *He noticed the full moon and knew it was time to go to sleep.*

4. *Mr. Baker sold eighteen of the sandwiches but had hoped to sell them all.*

5. *One large but sparsely populated country is Australia.* Or use *and.*

6. *The new restaurant is popular and does not accept reservations.* Or use *but.*

7. *My neighbor and Alex ride the bus to work each day.* (Use a plural verb with the plural subject.)

8. *The history of the flute is interesting but is not commonly known.* Or use *and.*

9. *Ruby bought the novel as soon as it was published but has not read it yet.*

10. *I saw Dennis at the grocery store and Miss Westin at the pharmacy.*

Skill 3 Clear Sentences

Lesson 1

There may be more than one correct way to edit some sentences.

1. *The result surprised the governor.* Avoid wordiness.

2. *Before she had lunch, the athlete was interviewed by Alice Johnson.* OR *Before Alice Johnson had lunch, she interviewed the athlete.* Avoid unclear pronoun reference.

3. *All the employees have asked their manager for an increase in pay.* Eliminate or change words that make the sentence unclear.

4. *The proprietor discreetly asked the customers to pay.* Eliminate or change words that make the sentence unclear.

5. *Our two choices were to postpone the meeting or to proceed as planned.* Avoid wordiness.

6. *The inexpensive newspaper is printed with a greasy ink,* OR *The newspaper is printed with an inexpensive, greasy ink.* Avoid unclear pronoun reference.

7. *The sunlight shone through the window.* Eliminate or change words that make the sentence unclear.

8. *Until jogger #10 suddenly raced ahead, she ran next to #3.* OR *Until she suddenly ran ahead, jogger #3 ran next to #10.* In the original sentence, it was not clear as to which jogger the pronoun "she" referred. Avoid unclear pronoun reference.

9. *The crowd of 85 people waited patiently.* Avoid wordiness.

10. *After he performed, the soloist met the singer.* OR *After the singer performed, he met the soloist.* Avoid unclear pronoun reference.

Lesson 2

There may be more than one correct way to edit some sentences.

1. *When they are young, many people dislike vegetables such as broccoli and cauliflower.* Move *when they are young* to a position where it clearly modifies *people.*

2. *As we reached the corner, the traffic light changed to red.* Reword the sentence to eliminate the dangling modifier, *Reaching the corner.*

3. Correct. *Exhausted by the long tour* modifies *we.*

4. *Forgetting his appointment, Albert gazed at the painting.* Move *forgetting his appointment* to a position where it clearly modifies *Albert.*

5. *When I spoke with you earlier, I asked you to pay the bill promptly.* Move *promptly* so that it clearly modifies the phrase, *pay the bill.*

6. *Waiting for the train, Rita discovered her watch had stopped.* Move *waiting for the train* to a position where it clearly modifies *Rita.*

7. *In the spring, Holland is covered with acres of blooming tulips.* Reword the sentence so that *blooming* modifies *tulips.*

8. Correct. This sentence consists of two complete ideas joined by *and* rather than a modifying phrase and one main idea.

9. *Mr. Alcorn bought three boxes of detergent on sale at the supermarket.* OR *At the supermarket, Mr. Alcorn bought three boxes of detergent on sale.* Move *on sale* so that it clearly modifies *boxes of detergent.*

10. *I brought home a kitten with a black spot on its nose.* Move the modifying phrase *with a black spot* ...closer to the word it modifies.

Lesson 3

1. *The concept of democracy was bold, innovative, and risky.* Change *involved some risk* to *risky* for parallel structure.

2. *Neither loss of appetite nor dizziness is a side-effect of her medication.* Change *to be dizzy* to *dizziness* for parallel structure.

3. *Bridging, budding, and clefting are three types of grafting familiar to most gardeners.* Change *To bridge* to *Bridging* for parallel structure.

4. *Major milestones in child development include learning to see, walk, and speak.* Change *speech* to *speak* for parallel structure.

5. *Training horses, flying, and writing were Beryl Markham's primary accomplishments.* Change *to write* to *writing* for parallel structure.

6. *Physicians strive to detect, cure, and prevent disease.* Change *the prevention of* to *prevent* for parallel structure.

7. *The safety of the passengers, the reliability of the equipment, and the efficiency of the system were the controller's greatest concerns.* Change *whether the system was efficient* to *the efficiency of the system* for parallel structure.

8. Correct. *Architecture, dance, photography, and travel* are parallel.

9. *Kim said the finest contributions of the twentieth century were the paper napkin, the ball point pen, and the disposable razor.* Change *to make a* to *the* for parallel structure.

10. *Firefighters need to possess physical strength, be able to work under pressure, and think quickly.* Change *thinking* to *think* for parallel structure.

Chapter 3   Mechanics
Skill 1 Capitalization

Lesson 1

1. **New Orleans** *is the largest city in the state of* **Louisiana.** Capitalize the names of places.

2. *My grandmother has always been especially fond of* **Chinese** *food.* Capitalize proper adjectives.

3. *Much* **Portuguese** *fish is exported to other European countries.* Capitalize proper adjectives.

4. *One of the most famous zoos in the world is located in* **San Diego,** *California.* Capitalize the names of places.

5. *Languages commonly spoken in Switzerland include* **German, French,** *English, and Italian.* Capitalize the names of languages.

6. *The trees along Main Street are maintained by the* **Village Improvement Society.** Capitalize the names of institutions.

7. Correct.

8. *On our trip to Washington, we visited the Senate and the* **House of Representatives.** Capitalize the names of institutions.

9. Correct. *Istanbul, Ankara, Izmir, and Turkey* are correctly capitalized.

10. *North, south, east, west* are only capitalized when they refer to a particular geographical region, not when they are used to indicate direction. *We left the Northeast and drove south to Miami, Florida.*

Lesson 2

1. *Each state is entitled to two* **senators** *and to a different number of* **representatives,** *according to its population.* Do not capitalize titles that are not used as part of a person's name.

2. *I saw* **Uncle** *Henry at the graduation ceremony.* Capitalize words such as *uncle* when they are used as part of a person's name.

3. Correct. The title, *Dr. Johnson* is correctly capitalized.

4. *We told Irene to speak to our* **mother** *about plans for the picnic.* Do not capitalize words expressing family relationships when they are not used as part of a person's name.

5. *The White House is located at 1600 Pennsylvania* **Avenue** *in Washington, D.C.* Capitalize the names of streets.

6. Correct. *Elm Street* is correctly capitalized.

7. *Our aunt's relatives asked* **Reverend** *Foster to perform the service.* Capitalize titles when they are used as part of a person's name.

8. Correct. *Williams Avenue* is correctly capitalized.

9. *I told Susan to ask* **Ms.** *Santos, the Director of Public Welfare, about the telephone call.* Capitalize the first letter of an abbreviation that stands for a title.

10. *This matter will have to be decided by* **Mayor** *Weston.* Capitalize titles when used with a person's name.

Lesson 3

1. *Heavy snowfalls in* **winter** *are not unusual in Maine.* Do not capitalize the seasons.

2. *The last day of the year is* **December** *31.* Capitalize the months.

3. *Nero was one of the cruelest rulers of the* **Roman Empire.** Capitalize names of organizations and institutions.

4. Correct. *World War II* is correctly capitalized.

5. *Michelangelo and Leonardo Da Vinci were two of the greatest artists of the* **Renaissance.** Capitalize the names of historical periods.

6. *The test begins at 9* **A.M.** Capitalize time abbreviations.

7. *Thanksgiving Day occurs on the fourth* **Thursday** *of November.* Capitalize days of the week.

8. **The Vietnam War** *took place during the 1960s and early 1970s.* Capitalize historical events.

9. Correct.

10. *New Year's* **Day** *is an occasion for visits and presents in Japan.* Capitalize holidays.

Skill 2 Punctuation

Lesson 1

1. *The talented, lively, and intelligent actress gave a marvelous television interview.* Do not use a comma between the last adjective in a series and the word it modifies.

2. *The major factors in the value of a house are size, location, and condition.* Use commas to separate items in a series.

3. *Tall, slender, graceful trees surround the clearing.* Do not use a comma between the last adjective in a series and the word it modifies.

4. Correct. Commas are used to separate items in a series.

5. *Participation in sports can increase the motivation, teamwork, and leadership abilities of many students.* Do not use a comma after *and* and before the last item in a series.

6. *Lisa bent down to examine a small, dark red shell on the beach.* Use a comma to separate an adjective that does not modify a second adjective in a series.

7. *We are interested in buying a car that has cruise control and power windows.* Do not use commas when there are fewer than three items in a series.

8. *The trembling, frightened bird sat on the window ledge.* Use a comma to separate an adjective that does not modify a second adjective in a series.

9. *Three popular breeds of cat are the Siamese, the Burmese, and the Persian.* Use commas to separate items in a series.

10. *When I am in New York, I will visit the Metropolitan Museum, the Bronx Zoo, the Empire State Building, and the World Trade Center.* Commas are used to separate items in a series, rather than *and*. When a coordinator like *and* occurs before the last item in a series, a comma is used before the coordinator.

Lesson 2

Note: The rule that governs all of these sentences is that a comma precedes the coordinator in a compound sentence.

1. *Our office recently purchased a new computer, and now many jobs can be finished more quickly.*

2. *Land prices in this town are rising quickly, for the area is extremely attractive to out-of-state residents.*

3. *The court will have to rule on Ms. Tarn's petition, or she will file an appeal.*

4. *Municipal zoos provide pleasure to many people, but the care of the animals has often been questioned.*

5. *You can buy the tools at the local hardware store or make a special trip into Madison to get them.* This is not a compound sentence, so no comma is needed.

6. *Many excavations in China are still in the planning stage, and archaeologists have hopes of discovering new treasures.*

7. Correct. The two ideas in the compound sentence are very short, and therefore, no comma is needed before the coordinator.

8. Correct.

9. *The price of gasoline will have to come down, or Americans will take fewer vacation trips this summer.*

10. Correct.

Lesson 3

1. *Honored guests, I would like to say a few words about the achievements of our principal speaker.* Use a comma after names or words of direct address.

2. Correct. A comma is used after an introductory phrase.

3. *Hank, I would like you to run for team captain.* Use a comma after names or words of direct address.

4. *When the heat was shut off in that building, the pipes froze in the sub-zero weather and burst.* Use a comma after a subordinate idea that appears at the beginning of a sentence.

5. *Yes, the train will arrive 45 minutes late.* Use a comma after an introductory word.

6. *However, we will be able to spend at least one day hiking this weekend.* Use a comma after an introductory word.

7. *Uncle Henry, I'd like to introduce my friend Tim.* Use a comma after names or words of direct address.

8. Correct. A comma is used after an introductory phrase.

9. *Moreover, we did not realize that we should have checked the route carefully before setting out.* Use a comma after an introductory word.

10. *No, he decided not to take that job.* Use a comma after an introductory word.

Lesson 4

1. *Susan Ramos, our class president, will address the assembly.* Use commas to set off a sentence interrupter.

2. *The musical West Side Story enjoyed a long run on Broadway.* Do not use commas if the word or phrase that describes a noun is essential to the meaning of the sentence.

3. *The roof, in my opinion, needs patching in several places.* Use commas to set off a sentence interrupter.

4. Correct. Commas are used to set off the sentence interrupter.

5. *The capital of Oregon, I believe, is Salem.* Use commas to set off a sentence interrupter.

6. *You will, I hope, ask for a raise within the next month.* Use commas to set off a sentence interrupter.

7. *These models, on the other hand, have automatic transmission.* Use commas to set off a sentence interrupter.

8. Correct. This sentence does not contain a sentence interrupter.

9. *The window, nevertheless, was open.* Use commas to set off a sentence interrupter.

10. Correct. Commas are used to set off the sentence interrupter.

Lesson 5

1. *World War II ended in Europe in May of 1945, but peace did not come in the Far East until August of that year.* Do not use a comma after a coordinator that joins two complete sentences.

2. Correct. This sentence is correctly punctuated.

3. *Mr. Rescigno will visit Boston, Providence, and Hartford.* Do not use a comma after *and* and before the last item in a series.

4. *Sandy bought crackers, cheese, and a head of lettuce at the store.* Do not use a comma before the first item in a series or before the last one.

5. *The fashion industry is centered in New York, and the entertainment industry is based in Hollywood.* Do not use a comma after a coordinator that joins two complete sentences.

6. *A short run and a relaxing swim were what we needed that day.* Do not use a comma with a compound subject.

7. *One of the most famous paintings in the world is called the Mona Lisa.* Do not use a comma between the subject and verb of a sentence.

8. *Mark Twain's novels and stories often contain clever, ironic humor.* Do not use a comma to separate an adjective from the noun it describes.

9. *The three dogs ran and played in the park.* Do not use commas with compound verbs.

10. Correct. This sentence is correctly punctuated.

Skill 3 Spelling

Lesson 1

1. *At lunchtime, only one of the **benches** in the park was empty.* The noun *bench* is made plural by adding *-es* to the singular form of the word.

2. ***Mysteries** are Larry's favorite type of bedtime reading.* The noun *mystery* ends in *y* preceded by a consonant. The plural is formed by replacing the *y* with *i* and adding *-es*.

3. *Even people who dislike most types of **fish** will eat tuna salad sandwiches. Fish* is a noun that is the same in both the singular and plural form.

4. *The hosts provided the **knives** and forks for the pot luck supper.* The plural of many nouns ending in *fe*, such as *knife*, is formed by changing the *f* to *v* and adding *-es*.

5. *After **plotting** out their route, the Jacksons left for vacation.* To form the *-ing* form of *plot*, double the final *t* before adding *-ing*.

6. *As a finishing touch, Julie **dotted** the i on her sign "Julie's Bakery—Open for Business."* To form the past tense of *dot*, double the final *t* and add *-ed*.

7. *Learning CPR can save **lives.*** The plural of many nouns ending in *fe*, such as *life*, is formed by changing the *f* to *v* and adding *-es*.

8. Correct. To form the *-ing* form of *wrap*, double the final *p* before adding *-ing*.

9. *The extra set of **keys** is hanging up near the kitchen sink.* Nouns that end in *y*, preceded by a vowel such as *key*, usually form their plurals by adding *-s*.

10. *Jackets made from the hides of **sheep** are popular in Colorado. Sheep* is a noun that is the same in both the singular and the plural form.

Lesson 2

1. *You buy your ticket and we will buy **ours.*** Do not use an apostrophe with a possessive pronoun.

2. *How much did **your** new bicycle cost, Jim?* Do not confuse the contraction *you're* with the possessive pronoun *your*.

3. *The **doctor's** office was closed.* An apostrophe is needed to show possession.

4. *Susan B. Anthony was an important figure in the struggle for **women's** rights.* Use an apostrophe with possessive nouns.

5. Correct. The apostrophe is correctly placed at the end of *states'*, a plural possessive noun.

6. *Did you ask mother which of these books were **hers**?* Do not use an apostrophe with a possessive pronoun.

7. *My cat likes to sleep on **its** back.* Do not confuse the contraction *it's* with the possessive pronoun *its*.

8. Correct. The singular possessive noun, *director's*, is correctly written.

9. *We asked Martha to put away the **children's** toys.* The possessive of the plural noun *children* is formed by the addition of *-'s*.

10. Correct. The apostrophe is correctly placed in the singular possessive noun, *orchestra*.

Lesson 3

1. ***It's** true that Thomas Jefferson and John Adams both died on the same day, July 4, 1826.* Use an apostrophe to form the contraction of *it is*.

2. *I'd like to borrow **your** copy of that novel.* Do not confuse the contraction *you're* with the possessive pronoun *your*.

3. ***Isn't** Peru located in South America?* The apostrophe is placed to show where letters have been omitted.

4. Correct. *He'd* is a contraction of *he would*.

5. ***I'm** very grateful for your recommendation.* Use an apostrophe to form the contraction of *I am*.

6. *We're sorry that we **didn't** see that play.* The apostrophe is placed to show where letters have been omitted.

7. Correct. *We've* is the contraction of *we have*.

8. *We found out that the Richardsons intend to sell **their** business.* Do not confuse the contraction *they're* with the possessive pronoun *their*.

9. Correct. *Aren't* is the contraction of *are not*.

10. ***Let's** all meet at the bus station at five o'clock.* Use an apostrophe to form the contraction of *let us*.

Lesson 4

1. *Mustard **complements** many different foods.*

2. *We told the instructor that our assignments were **already** completed.*

3. *I **heard** that Richard had a very successful interview.*

4. *When the flight was called, the passengers boarded the **plane**.*

5. Correct. Principle is correctly spelled.

6. *A major issue now is the proper disposal of nuclear **wastes**.*

7. *Usually **there** are nine innings in a baseball game.*

8. *Except for a few **minor** errors, the news article was accurate.*

9. *Does this car have reliable **brakes**?*

10. *An amendment will be required to **alter** the by-laws.*

Lesson 5

1. Change *boundry* to *boundary*.
2. Change *cheif* to *chief*.
3. Change *conceil* to *conceal*.
4. Change *criticizm* to *criticism*.
5. Change *interupt* to *interrupt*.
6. Change *liesure* to *leisure*.
7. Change *paralel* to *parallel*.
8. Change *posession* to *possession*.
9. Change *seperate* to *separate*.
10. Change *sucessful* to *successful*.

Chapter 4   Editing Paragraphs

Lesson 1

1. **(5)** *Usage / Subject–Verb Agreement / Sentence Correction.* Change *was* to *were*. The plural subject, *performances*, requires a plural verb, *were*.

2. **(2)** *Mechanics / Comma / Sentence Correction.* Insert a comma after *Corps*. Use a comma after a subordinate idea when it appears first in a sentence.

3. **(5)** *Sentence Structure / Subordination / Sentence Correction.* No error in the sentence.

4. **(3)** *Sentence Structure / Run-On / Coordination / Sentence Correction.* Insert a semicolon after *remark*. Use a semicolon with the coordinator *that is* to join two complete ideas in a compound sentence.

5. **(4)** *Sentence Structure / Coordination / Sentence Correction.* Insert *for instance* after semi-colon followed by a comma. Use a coordinator that shows an example: They must *write accurately* is an example of one of the skills journalists must master.

6. **(2)** *Usage / Subject-Verb Agreement / Sentence Revision. Banana but tastes.* The singular subject *plantain* requires a singular verb *tastes*.

7. **(3)** *Sentence Structure / Coordination / Construction Shift.* Use a coordinator that shows a conclusion. The intent of the sentence is to show that the presence of rain led Jean to refrain from watering the garden.

8. **(5)** *Usage/Verb Tense/Sentence Correction.* Change *leaves* to *left.* Use the past tense of the irregular verb *leave* to show action that happened in the past.

9. **(4)** *Mechanics/Comma/Sentence Revision. If properly cared for, it.* Commas are used to set off sentence interrupters. The words *if properly cared for* add information about *this plant.*

10. **(1)** *Sentence Structure/Coordination/ Construction Shift. However.* A transition that shows contrast is needed. The intent of the sentence is to show a difference between what pandas are and what they are thought to be.

Lesson 2

1. **(4)** *Usage/Subject–Verb Agreement/ Sentence Correction.* The singular indefinite pronoun *one* takes a singular verb.

2. **(3)** *Sentence Structure/Subordination/ Construction Shift.* When ideas of unequal rank are joined by a subordinator, *before,* do not use a coordinator.

3. **(4)** *Sentence Structure/Run-on Sentences/ Sentence Revision.* A run-on sentence can be corrected by using a semicolon at the end of the first idea. A comma should follow the coordinator, *thus.*

4. **(5)** *No correction is necessary.*

5. **(4)** *Usage/Relative Pronouns/Sentence Revision.* Use the relative pronoun *who* to refer to a person or people.

6. **(4)** *Mechanics/Capitalization/Sentence Correction.* A proper noun should always be capitalized.

7. **(2)** *Mechanics/Punctuation/Commas/ Sentence Revision.* In a series of three or more items, use a comma after each item.

8. **(5)** *Mechanics/Punctuation/Commas/ Sentence Revision.* An interrupter that is not essential to the main idea of the sentence is set off by commas.

9. **(4)** *Sentence Structure/Parallel Structure/ Sentence Correction.* All items in a listing must be in the same form.

10. **(3)** *Mechanics/Capitalization/Sentence Correction.* Proper adjectives are always capitalized.

Lesson 3

1. **(2)** *Usage/Subject–Verb Agreement/ Sentence Revision.* A plural subject, *stations,* must use a plural verb.

2. **(5)** *Usage/Verb Tense—Clues Within Paragraph/Sentence Revision.* Use the past tense of the irregular verb *drive* to show action that took place in the past.

3. **(3)** *Usage/Verb Tense—Irregular Verbs/Sentence Correction.* The past participle of the irregular verb *build* is *built.*

4. **(5)** *Usage/Verb Tense/Subject–Verb Agreement/Construction Shift.* The revised sentence uses that past-tense helping verb *was* with the past participle of the main verb *show* to read *was shown.*

5. **(4)** *Usage/Pronoun Reference/Sentence Revision.* The pronoun *they* does not have a clear antecedent.

6. **(4)** *Usage/Subject–Verb Agreement/ Sentence Correction.* When a compound subject is joined by *and,* a plural verb is used.

7. **(5)** *Usage/Verb Tense/Sentence Revision.* The phrase *in those days* is a clue that the verb should be in the past tense.

8. **(4)** *Usage/Subject–Verb Agreement/ Sentence Correction. Few* is a plural pronoun, which must be used with a plural verb.

9. **(2)** *Usage/Subject–Verb Agreement— Inverted Sentence Structure/Sentence Revision.* A singular subject *notion* must use a singular verb *is.*

10. **(4)** *Usage/Pronoun Shift/Sentence Correction.* The pronouns in a sentence must agree in person.

Lesson 4

1. **(2)** *Sentence Structure/Run-on/Sentence Correction.* Eliminate the comma splice by using a semicolon after the first complete idea.

2. **(4)** *Sentence Structure/Clarity/Sentence Revision.* Add and reorder words to show that *capable of simultaneously producing both melody and harmony* modifies *piano.*

3. **(3)** *Sentence Structure/Parallel Structure/ Sentence Correction.* All items that are listed in a series should be in the same form.

4. **(1)** *Sentence Structure/Clarity/Subordination/Construction Shift.* A pronoun must clearly refer to its antecedent.

5. **(4)** *Sentence Structure/Run-on Sentence/ Sentence Revision.* This is a run-on sentence. Use a comma and a connecting word to make it a compound sentence.

6. **(5)** *Sentence Structure/Coordination/ Sentence Revision.* Use a coordinator that contrasts one idea with another.

7. **(3)** *Sentence Structure/Sentence Fragment/Sentence Revision.* The word *although* makes this group of words an incomplete idea.

8. **(3)** *Sentence Structure/Coordination/ Sentence Correction.* This sentence is not compound. The comma should be deleted to show that *the grand piano* is the subject for both parts of the sentence.

9. **(4)** *Sentence Structure/Subordinations/ Construction Shift. Grand pianos are usually about nine feet in length although they occasionally are built in a smaller size which measures five feet.* The revised sentence requires a subordinator that contrasts one idea with another. *Although* has this meaning.

10. **(5)** *Sentence Structure/Fragment/ Sentence Revision.* When a subordinate idea comes first in a sentence, it is followed by a comma.

Lesson 5

1. **(1)** *Mechanics/Comma/Sentence Interrupter/Sentence Correction.* When a word describing a noun is essential to the meaning of the sentence, it is not set off by commas. The word *poultry* is essential because without it the meaning of *term* would be unclear.

2. **(3)** *Mechanics/Apostrophe/Possessives/ Sentence Revision.* The plural noun *countries* does not indicate ownership and does not take an apostrophe.

3. **(2)** *Mechanics/Commas/Punctuation/ Sentence Correction.* In a series of three or more items, commas are used to separate the items.

4. **(5)** *Mechanics/Spelling/Sentence Correction.* The contraction *they're* (for *they are*) is correctly spelled.

5. **(5)** *Mechanics/Capitalization/Sentence Revision.* Proper nouns are always capitalized.

6. **(4)** *Mechanics/Spelling/Sentence Correction. Varieties* is frequently misspelled.

7. **(3)** *Mechanics/Capitalization/Sentence Correction.* Do not capitalize a noun that is modified by a proper adjective.

8. **(3)** *Mechanics/Compound Sentences/ Sentence Revision.* When punctuating a compound sentence, a comma is needed before the coordinating word.

9. **(5)** *Mechanics/Capitalization/Sentence Correction.* Names of holidays are always capitalized.

10. **(4)** *Mechanics/Spelling/Homonyms/ Sentence Revision.* Use the possessive pronoun *their* to show on whose farms poultry is raised. *There* is used as an expletive or to mean "in that place."

Lesson 6

1. **(2)** *Usage/Subject–Verb Agreement/ Sentence Correction. Everyone* is a singular indefinite pronoun and takes the singular verb *has.*

2. **(4)** *Sentence Structure/Subordination/ Construction Shift. Paper, as we know it, did not exist before the nineteenth century.* The revised sentence makes the relationship between ideas clearer.

3. **(2)** *Sentence Structure/Clarity/Sentence Correction.* Avoid wordiness. In this case, *chief* means the same thing as *main.*

4. **(1)** *Mechanics/Punctuation/Sentence Revision.* When two modifiers (*fine* and *expensive*) describe a noun (*writing paper*), separate the modifiers by a comma.

5. **(3)** *Sentence Structure/Run-on Sentence/ Sentence Revision.* Eliminate the comma splice by placing a period after the first complete idea.

6. **(4)** *Usage/Verb Tense/Sentence Correction. In 1869* tells you the action took place in the past. Use the past tense, *began.*

7. **(5)** *Usage/Pronoun Reference/Sentence Revision.* Use the relative pronoun *which* or *that* to refer to a thing.

8. **(2)** *Sentence Structure/Coordination/ Construction Shift.* Use a coordinator that shows an example. The availability of books, magazines, and newspapers is an example of the ways in which paper has altered the spread of information.

9. **(3)** *Mechanics/Spelling/Sentence Correction. Abundant* is frequently misspelled.

10. **(5)** *Mechanics/Capitalization/Sentence Revision.* Always capitalize proper nouns; *United States* is a proper noun.

Half-Length Practice Test

1. *Sentence Structure/Comma Splice/ Sentence Correction.* **(2)** Do not use a comma to separate two ideas that could stand alone. The error is corrected by writing two sentences.

2. *Usage/Verb Tense/Construction Shift.* **(2)** *You should read the guarantee carefully before you buy a product.* The singular subject, *you,* requires a singular verb, *buy.*

3. *Mechanics/Capitalization/Proper Names/ Sentence Correction.* **(1)** Since *law* is not used here as part of the name of a specific law, there is no need to capitalize it.

4. *Usage/Subject–Verb Agreement/Sentence Revision.* **(3)** The relative pronoun, (*the one*) *who*, requires a singular verb, *stands*.

5. *Mechanics/Spelling/Homonyms/Sentence Correction.* **(2)** Be careful not to confuse *whether* and *weather*. He did not know *whether* or not the weekend *weather* would be good.

6. *Sentence Structure/Fragment/Sentence Revision.* **(3)** Be especially careful that a sentence has both subject and verb when you see "ing" words. The fragment is corrected by supplying a subject, *it*, and a verb, *must tell*.

7. *Sentence Structure/Run-on/Sentence Revision.* **(4)** When two complete ideas are joined by a connecting word, make sure to use a comma before the *or, and, nor, for,* or *but.*

8. *Usage/Pronoun Shift/Sentence Correction.* **(4)** Use pronouns consistently. The use of *you're* should be followed by the use of *you have*.

9. *Mechanics/Punctuation/Comma After Introduction/Sentence Revision.* **(4)** A comma is needed after *purchase* to indicate the end of the introduction to the sentence.

10. *Usage/Subject–Verb Agreement/Expletive/Sentence Correction.* **(2)** The plural subject, *ways*, requires a plural verb, *are*.

11. *Sentence Structure/Coordination/Construction Shift.* **(5)** *The Armed Forces, for example, offer training and work experience for many jobs.* The new construction eliminates unnecessary words.

12. *Sentence Structure/Fragments/Sentence Revision.* **(4)** Use a semicolon to join two sentences. Since *when he joins the Navy* is not a complete sentence and cannot stand alone, the semicolon should not be used. A comma should not be used either because the words following *when* are essential to the meaning of the sentence.

13. *Mechanics/Punctuation/Comma between Items in a Series/Construction Shift.* **(1)** *Students at cooking schools have to pay for tuition, room, and board.* Separate three or more items in a series with commas.

14. *Usage/Pronoun Shift/Sentence Revision.* **(4)** Use pronouns consistently. Here, *they* is used to replace *students*.

15. *Mechanics/Punctuation/Unnecessary Comma/Sentence Correction.* **(1)** No comma is used because the *and* joins two verbs, not two sentences: *learns cooking skills* and *is expected to spend a certain amount of time in the Navy.*

16. *Usage/Verb Tense—Sequence of Tenses/Sentence Correction.* **(4)** Make sure tenses follow in a logical order. The phrase, *When...is over*, should be followed by *may choose*.

17. *Usage/Verb Tense/Clues within Sentence/Sentence Correction.* **(2)** Use clues to verb tense within a sentence. The word *now* indicates the need for the present tense, *has*.

18. *Sentence Structure/Fragment/Sentence Revision.* **(3)** Every sentence needs a subject and a verb that agrees with it. Here, the implied subject is *he*; replacing *deciding* with *will decide* provides the verb.

19. *Mechanics/Apostrophe/Spelling/Frequently Misspelled Words Benefit/Sentence Correction.* **(5)** Misspellings often result from the fact that *a, e, i* and *u* may all make the same sound, that made by the second *e* in *benefits*.

20. *Usage/Subject–Verb Agreement/Inverted Structure/Sentence Revision.* **(5)** Even when subject and verb are reversed, the subject requires a verb that agrees with it. The singular subject, *barcode*, requires a singular verb, *is*.

21. *Sentence Structure/Run-on/Sentence Correction.* **(2)** Use a comma to separate two complete ideas when they are joined by the connectors *and, but, or, nor, for, yet.*

22. *Sentence Structure/Subordination/Construction Shift.* **(2)** *Some stores even have computers with voices that say the name and price of the item as it passes through the scanner.* The new construction avoids repetition of *voices*.

23. *Usage/Verb Tense—Sequence of Tenses/Sentence Correction.* **(5)** The present tense, *is*, is required to remain consistent with the present tense used within the sentence and throughout the paragraph.

24. *Mechanics/Capitalization/Proper Adjective/Sentence Correction.* **(2)** Capitalize adjectives that refer to proper names. Here, the adjective *Spanish* refers to the name of a country, *Spain*.

25. *Mechanics/Spelling/Homonyms/Sentence Correction.* **(5)** Use *your* here to indicate possession.

26. *Sentence Structure/Parallelism/Sentence Correction.* **(5)** The connector *and* is used to connect ideas of equal importance in similar form....*put and type...*

27. *Usage/Verb Tense—Clues in Paragraph/Sentence Revision.* **(3)** Use verbs consistently within a paragraph. Here, the present tense, *are printed,* is required to remain consistent with the present tense used throughout the paragraph.

28. *Sentence Structure/Parallelism/Sentence Revision.* **(5)** Express similar ideas in similar form....*lines shorter, inventories easier,...prices lower.*

Full-length Practice Test

1. *Mechanics/Capitalization/Titles of People/Sentence Correction.* **(4)** Capitalize a title when it comes before a person's name.

2. *Sentence Structure/Fragments/Sentence Correction.* **(1)** Make a sentence from the fragment by providing an appropriate subject, *He.*

3. *Sentence Structure/Modification-Dangling Modifier/Sentence Revision.* **(5)** *He,* not *something, was returning home.* Make sure you keep what is described as close as you can to its description.

4. *Usage/Ambiguous Reference/Construction Shift.* **(3)** *Dr. Fleming made penicillin from the mold.* When you use pronouns such as *this* or *it,* make sure it is clear to what they refer.

5. *Mechanics/Punctuation/Comma after Introductory Elements/Sentence Revision.* **(4)** Use a comma to set off the words that introduce the subject, *many illnesses.*

6. *Mechanics/Punctuation/Apostrophe in Contraction/Spelling/Homonyms/Sentence Correction.* **(4)** An apostrophe is needed to indicate a contraction and take the place of *i* in *it is. It's* is easily confused with *its,* which is used to show possession.

7. *Usage/Verb Tense—Clues within Sentence/Sentence Correction.* **(5)** Keep verb tense consistent. The present tense is used for *doesn't,* and present tense should be used for *can cause.*

8. *Mechanics/Spelling/Homonyms/Troublesome Possessives/Sentence Correction.* **(1)** *Your* is the possessive; *you're* is the contraction for *you are.*

9. *Usage/Verb Tense—Clues to Tense in Paragraph/Sentence Revision.* **(2)** Make sure verb tense is consistent throughout the paragraph. The paragraph cautions you about use of penicillin today.

10. *Sentence Structure/Clarity/Subordination/Construction Shift.* **(4)** *Anyone who begins a job training program soon discovers that each occupation has its own technical language.* Eliminate unnecessary words like *in this day and age.*

11. *Usage/Subject–Verb Agreement/Sentence Correction.* **(5)** No correction.

12. *Usage/Pronoun Reference—Relative Pronoun/Sentence Correction.* **(2)** Use *who* when referring to people; *which* refers to things.

13. *Usage/Verb Tense Errors/Verb Form/Sentence Correction.* **(5)** Learn the forms of irregular verbs like *draw: He draws; he drew; he has drawn.*

14. *Mechanics/Punctuation/Commas/Construction Shift.* **(4)** *A machine tool operator, who cuts and shapes metal, needs to be able to talk about his or her machine.* Set off words that are not essential to the meaning of the sentence with commas. Here, *who cuts and shapes metal* is not essential.

15. *Usage/Subject–Verb Agreement—Connectives Other Than And/Sentence Revision.* **(1)** Don't be fooled by connectors such as *like* or *unlike.* The singular subject, *welder,* requires a singular verb, *works.*

16. *Mechanics/Spelling/Homonyms—Piece/Peace/Sentence Correction.* **(5)** When checking spelling, watch out for words that sound alike, but have different spellings, such as *piece/peace.*

17. *Sentence Structure/Fragments/Sentence Correction.* **(2)** Correct the fragment by providing a verb, *need,* for the subject, *medical secretaries and nurses.*

18. *Mechanics/Punctuation/Comma After Introduction/Sentence Revision.* **(2)** Use a comma to set off an introductory dependent clause (a word group that could not stand alone). Use semicolons to join two sentences.

19. *Usage/Pronoun Shift/Sentence Correction.* **(1)** Since the pronoun, *you,* was used in the previous sentence, continue to use *you.*

20. *Usage/Expletive/Sentence Revision.* **(5)** The plural subject, *businesses,* requires a plural verb, *are.*

21. *Sentence Structure/Improper Subordination/Sentence Correction.* **(1)** Choose words such as *Because* that show how one part of a sentence is related to another. *Because* (not *Although*) companies are *trying to make profits, it's important...*

22. *Mechanics/Punctuation/Commas/Sentence Correction.* **(1)** When two expressions with the same function are side by side, separate them with commas. Here, *those gifts of modern science* is another way of saying *Computers.*

23. *Sentence Structure/Subordination/Construction Shift.* **(3)** *Suppose I need a typewriter ribbon made by the Jones Halo Company.* The new construction is more concise.

24. *Usage/Subject–Verb Agreement—Neither/Nor/Sentence Revision.* **(2)** The singular nouns, *store* and *one,* joined by *neither/nor* are considered a singular subject and require a singular verb, *has.*

25. *Mechanics/Capitalization/Dates/Sentence Correction.* **(1)** Capitalize the names of holidays such as *Valentine's Day.*

26. *Mechanics/Spelling/Homonyms—Their/There/Sentence Correction.* **(1)** Don't confuse *their,* the possessive, with *there,* referring to a place.

27. *Mechanics/Capitalization/Sentence Correction.* **(5)** Keep tense consistent. The story about the ribbons, begun several sentences before, is being told in the present tense.

28. *Mechanics/Punctuation/Commas/Sentence Revision.* **(5)** Commas are needed to separate the different items in a series. A comma is used after the first item, between items, and before the *and* of the last item.

29. *Sentence Structure/Coordination/Subordination/Sentence Revision.* **(3)** Connectors such as *and, but, or,* and *nor* are used to connect two subject–verb structures that could stand alone. *If you're planning on buying a house* could not stand alone, and should be set off from the subject, *you,* with a comma.

30. *Sentence Structure/Run-on/Sentence Revision.* **(2)** Do not simply run together two subject–verb structures that could each stand alone. Separate with a connecting word, a semicolon, or, as in this case, a period.

31. *Mechanics/Capitalization/Titles of People/Sentence Correction.* **(5)** Capitalize titles, such as *Uncle* or *Grandma,* when they come before the person's name.

32. *Usage/Subject-Verb Agreement—Noun-Verb Pairs/Sentence Revision.* **(2)** The plural subject, *down payment and each monthly payment,* requires a plural verb, *are.*

33. *Sentence Structure/Parallelism/Sentence Correction.* **(4)** Don't omit necessary words. The connector, *and,* should join two similar word groups, *you pay...* and *you write....*

34. *Mechanics/Homonyms/Spelling/Sentence Correction.* **(4)** *You're* means *you are. Your* is used to show possession or relationship.

35. *Sentence Structure/Subordination/Construction Shift.* **(5)** *You might be one of the people with a poor credit rating, for instance, who may not be able to get one.* Answer 5 is the only answer that combines both sentences using the correct relative pronoun *who* to refer back to *people.*

36. *Sentence Structure/Run-on/Sentence Revision.* **(4)** Two subject–verb structures that could stand alone are joined, so place a comma before the connector, *but.*

37. *Usage/Verb Tense—Form/Sentence Correction.* **(2)** Learn the irregular form of verbs such as to rise: it rises; it rose; it has risen.

38. *Usage/Verb Tense—Clues within Paragraph/Sentence Revision.* **(2)** The present tense, *do,* is consistent with that used throughout the paragraph.

39. *Sentence Structure/Coordination/Semicolon between Independent Clauses/Sentence Revision.* **(4)** Omit the connector, *and,* when you use a semicolon to join two subject–verb structures.

40. *Sentence Structure/Subordination/Parallelism/Construction Shift.* **(5)** *There are many different data processing jobs and training programs.* Choice 5 combines both sentences using a few words. Remember to keep the two word groups similar in form.

41. *Mechanics/Capitalization/Proper Names/Sentence Correction.* **(1)** Capitalize the word *company* only if it appears as part of a name, such as *Smith Company, Inc.*

42. *Mechanics/Spelling/Frequently Misspelled Words–Desirable/Sentence Correction.* **(2)** Remember to drop the silent *e* before you add an ending starting with a vowel.

43. *Sentence Structure/Parallelism/Sentence Revision.* **(2)** Keep similar ideas in similar form. Three things are required: *time, effort, accuracy.*

44. *Usage/Ambiguous Pronoun Reference/ Sentence Correction.* **(4)** It is unclear to what *one* refers. The error is corrected by supplying a specific term, *skill.*

45. *Usage/Pronoun Shift/Sentence Revision.* **(2)** Keep pronouns consistent. Don't shift from *you* to *one.*

46. *Usage/Pronoun Shift/Vague Pronoun Reference/Construction Shift.* **(1)** *As long as you have your equivalency diploma, you will find a training program.* The new construction makes it clear what you will find.

47. *Sentence Structure/Fragment/Sentence Correction.* **(1)** The fragment is corrected by eliminating *Even if* and supplying a subject–verb structure that can stand alone: *You may have to work...*

48. *Sentence Structure/Run-on/Comma between Independent Clauses/Sentence Correction.* **(3)** Place a comma before the connecting word, *but,* joining two subject–verb structures that can stand alone.

49. *Sentence Structure/Subordination/ Coordination/Construction Shift* **(5)** *Although people are responsible for most computer errors, computers do sometimes cause the problems.* The word *Although* makes the new construction effective by signaling the relationship between the two ideas.

50. *Sentence Structure/Subject–Verb Agreement/Inverted Structure/Sentence Revision.* **(4)** The plural subject, *electronic parts,* requires a plural verb, *are,* despite the fact that the usual subject–verb order is reversed.

51. *Mechanics/Capitalization/Proper Names/Sentence Correction.* **(5)** Capitalize the names of countries.

52. *Usage/Pronoun References—Agreement with Antecedent/Sentence Revision.* **(4)** A pronoun can only be used to replace another word. Here, the pronoun *they* does not replace any word that has already been used.

53. *Sentence Structure/Coordination/ Sentence Correction.* **(5)** The sentence is correct and avoids being a run-on because of the semicolon separating the two subject–verb structures.

54. *Usage/Verb Tense—Clues within Paragraph/Subject–Verb Agreement/ Sentence Correction.* **(4)** In remaining consistent with the present tense used throughout the paragraph, the singular subject, *Weather,* requires a singular verb, *causes.*

55. *Usage/Subject–Verb Agreement— Interrupting Phrase/Sentence Revision.* **(1)** The sentence correctly pairs the singular subject, *group,* with a singular verb, *is made.*

Simulated Test —
Part 1

1. *Sentence Structure/Run-On/Sentence Revision.* **(5)** Don't run together two ideas that could each stand alone. The error is corrected by separating the ideas with a semicolon.

2. *Usage/Subject–Verb Agreement/ Noun–Verb Pairs/Construction Shift.* **(4)** *Careers, hobbies, and nutrition are among the numerous topics covered.* The plural subject, *Careers, hobbies, and nutrition,* requires a plural verb, *are.*

3. *Usage/Subject–Verb Agreement/ Interrupting Phrase/Sentence Revision.* **(1)** The plural subject, *Several,* requires plural verb, *deal,* despite the interrupting phrase, *of the publications.*

4. *Sentence Structure/Fragment/Sentence Correction.* **(2)** The sentence requires a subject and a verb to be complete. The pronoun *one* is the subject; replacing *being* with *is* provides the verb.

5. *Usage/Pronoun Reference—Agreement with Antecedent/Sentence Correction.* **(5)** Make sure that pronouns agree with the words they replace. *Their,* not *your,* agrees with *those.*

6. *Sentence Structure/Fragment/Sentence Revision.* **(2)** A subject–verb structure introduced by *If* cannot stand alone.

7. *Mechanics/Punctuation/Commas between Items in a Series/Sentence Revision.* **(5)** Three or more items in a series should be separated by commas.

8. *Mechanics/Spelling/Troublesome Homonyms/Sentence Correction.* **(1)** *Your* and *you're* sound alike but have different meanings. *You're going to spend your money.*

9. *Mechanics/Capitalization/Places/ Addresses/Sentence Correction.* **(4)** Capitalize the names of places, such as states, counties, and countries.

10. *Usage/Subject–Verb Agreement/ Connectives other than And/Sentence Correction.* **(1)** The singular subject, *alcohol*, requires a singular verb, *plays*, despite the connective, *as well as*.

11. *Sentence Structure/Subordination/ Construction Shift.* **(4)** *Unfortunately, about eleven teens die each day because of driving while drunk.* The words *because of* convey the same meaning as the original sentence's words, *results in*.

12. *Sentence Structure/Run-on/Sentence Correction.* **(4)** Use a semicolon to separate complete ideas connected by *however*.

13. *Usage/Subject–Verb Agreement/Neither-Nor/Sentence Correction.* **(2)** Plural nouns joined by *neither/nor* require a plural verb.

14. *Mechanics/Spelling/Frequently Misspelled Words/Sentence Correction.* **(5)** Remember the soft *c* in *licensing* and the single *l* in *eliminate*.

15. *Usage/Verb Tense—Sequence of Tenses/Sentence Correction.* **(4)** Some sentences contain words such as *after* or *before* that provide clues about the order of tenses. *After more studies have been done...requires the future tense, it will become...*

16. *Sentence Structure/Subordination/ Construction Shift.* **(5)** *Then perhaps we can find a more consistent way to fight the nation's number one killer of teenagers, drunk driving accidents.*

17. *Sentence Structure/Dangling Modifiers/ Sentence Revision.* **(5)** Keep a description next to what is being described. It is *these areas*, not *weary travelers*, that have *bathrooms and restaurants*.

18. *Usage/Pronoun Reference/Agreement with Antecedent/Sentence Correction.* **(5)** *They* is used correctly to replace *these areas*, from the preceding sentence.

19. *Sentence Structure/Parallelism/Sentence Correction.* **(5)** Similar ideas should be expressed in similar form....*museums, ski resorts, and amusement parks.*

20. *Mechanics/Spelling/Troublesome Possessives/Homonyms/Sentence Correction.* **(5)** Don't confuse the possessive *their* with *there*, which often refers to a location.

21. *Mechanics/Punctuation/Comma after Introductory Dependent Clause/Sentence Correction.* **(2)** Use a comma to separate the subject of a sentence from the subject–verb structure that precedes it.

22. *Usage/Pronoun Reference—Ambiguous Reference/Sentence Revision.* **(3)** Make sure it is clear what word a pronoun replaces. It refers not to *the number...on the screen*, but to *that number on the keyboard*.

23. *Sentence Structure/Subordination/ Modification/Construction Shift.* **(2)** *Without a computer, you undoubtedly could have found the same information, but it would have taken more time and energy.*

24. *Mechanics/Capitalization/Proper Name/Sentence Correction.* **(5)** *Consumer* is properly capitalized when contained in the name of a magazine and not capitalized when describing a general type of magazine.

25. *Usage/Verb Tense—Clues to Tense in Paragraph/Sentence Revision.* **(2)** *Have been selected* is consistent with the tense used earlier.

26. *Mechanics/Frequently Misspelled Words/Homonyms—Principle/Sentence Correction.* **(2)** *Principle* and *principal* sound alike but have different meanings. *The principle behind how it works is the principal thing to remember for the test.*

27. *Sentence Structure/Comma Splice/ Sentence Revision.* **(2)** Two complete ideas cannot be separated solely by a comma. Here, a semicolon is used to correct the error.

28. *Usage/Pronoun Reference/Sentence Correction.* **(3)** In the original, there is confusion as to whether *its* refers to the light-detecting or the radiation type of detector.

29. *Mechanics/Punctuation/Comma after Introductory Elements/Sentence Correction.* **(3)** Separate an introductory group of words from the subject it precedes with a comma.

30. *Sentence Structure/Fragment/Sentence Revision.* **(2)** The independent clause requires a subject and a verb to be complete. The noun *signal* is the subject; replacing *warning* with *warns* provides the verb.

31. *Usage/Relative Pronoun/Sentence Correction.* **(3)** *Which* is used to refer to things; *Who* is used to refer to people, as in this sentence *sleepers.*

32. *Usage/Subject–Verb Agreement/Noun–Verb Pairs/Construction Shift.* **(2)** *U.S. Immigration laws appear frequently in today's news.* The plural subject, *laws,* requires a plural verb, *appear.*

33. *Usage Verb Tense—Clues within Sentence/Sentence Revision.* **(2)** Clues to tense within the sentence, the words *For many years,* as well as clues throughout the paragraph, indicate that *have been* should be used.

34. *Sentence Structure/Subordination/Construction Shift.* **(3)** *In 1790, Congress passed a ruling that anyone who had lived in the U.S. for two years could become a citizen.*

35. *Sentence Structure/Run-on/Comma Splice/Sentence Revision.* **(5)** Don't use a comma to separate two ideas that could stand alone. Here, the second idea is made dependent on the first.

36. *Mechanics/Punctuation/Overuse of Commas/Sentence Revision.* **(3)** A comma should not be used because it interrupts the flow of thought.

37. *Mechanics/Capitalization/Sentence Correction.* **(2)** Capitalize the name of high government organizations, such as Congress.

38. *Mechanics/Capitalization/Titles/Sentence Correction.* **(1)** Capitalize a title when it appears before a particular name.

39. *Sentence Structure/Coordination/Sentence Correction.* **(5)** The word *both* indicates that *and,* not *yet,* is the correct connecting word.

40. *Usage/Subject–Verb Agreement/Expletive/Sentence Revision.* **(2)** The plural subject, *ways,* requires a plural verb, *are.*

41. *Mechanics/Punctuation/Appositive/Sentence Modifier/Sentence Correction.* **(2)** Use a comma to set off nonessential phrases such as *for example* from the rest of the sentence.

42. *Usage/Verb Form/Sentence Revision.* **(4)** *To show* is an irregular verb. *He shows; he showed; he was shown.*

43. *Mechanics/Capitalization/Dates/Sentence Correction.* **(3)** Capitalize only the names of specific holidays.

44. *Sentence Structure/Parallelism/Coordination/Sentence Revision.* **(2)** Express similar ideas joined by *or* or *and* in similar form....*going to a ballgame* or *visiting an aquarium....*

45. *Sentence Structure/Modification/Sentence Correction.* **(5)** *You* is correctly placed after the phrase, *By asking a few simple questions in your letter.* It is *you,* not the *child,* who asks the questions.

46. *Usage/Subject–Verb Agreement/Interrupting Phrase/Sentence Correction.* **(3)** The singular subject, *means,* requires a singular verb, *is.* Don't be confused by singular subjects that appear to be plural because they end in "s."

47. *Sentence Structure/Subordination/Construction Shift.* **(1)** *If a child who respects you sees you writing frequently, he or she will believe that you are earnest about the value of this activity.*

48. *Mechanics/Spelling/Frequently Misspelled Words/Sentence Correction.* **(1)** *Pastime* is on the list of frequently misspelled words.

49. *Usage/Verb Tense/Sentence Correction.* **(4)** The paragraph is written in the simple past tense. The past tense of *go* is *went.*

50. *Sentence Structure/Parallelism/Sentence Revision.* **(3)** The sentence lists types of performances included in a variety show. *Performers involved in acrobatics* should be changed to *acrobatics* to match the form of the other items in the list. The commas go between the items in the list and before the *and* of the last item.

51. *Mechanics/Punctuation/Comma/Sentence Correction.* **(4)** When more than one word is used to describe a noun, a comma is used between the descriptive words. A comma is never placed between the noun and the descriptive word directly in front of it (that is, the following would be incorrect: *Ragtime was a new, rhythmic, music with a lively sound.*)

52. *Mechanics/Punctuation/Commas/Capitalization/Sentence Corrections.* **(5)** No correction is necessary. The words of the song are appropriately capitalized, and the group of words providing the year that the song was written is correctly punctuated.

53. *Sentence Structure/Subordination/Construction Shift.* **(5)** *Although* is a word with the same meaning as *even though* which is used to indicate contrast. When *although* is used after the main part of the sentence, no comma is used before it. The answers with *but* and *however* are not correctly punctuated and would be examples of run-on sentences. The answers with *since* and *because* are incorrect because they illogically explain that the song swept the country *because* there was no nationwide radio network to make it widely known. *Sweeped* in (1) is also an incorrect past tense form of *sweep.*

54. *Usage/Subject–Verb Agreement/Sentence Revision.* **(2)** Were is used to agree with the plural subject marches. The past tense is used because the other verbs in the paragraph are in the past tense.

55. *Usage/Verb Tense/Sentence Revision.* **(5)** *Wrote,* the simple past tense of *write,* is used because the paragraph is written in the simple past tense to indicate actions completed in the past. A comma goes before *including* to indicate nonessential information which is added on to the sentence.

Simulated Test – Part II

Introduction to Holistic Scoring

The following *GED Essay Scoring Guide* provides a general description of the characteristics found in GED essays that are scored by the Holistic Method.

GED ESSAY SCORING GUIDE

Papers will show *some* or *all* of the following characteristics.

Upper-half papers make clear a definite purpose, pursued with varying degrees of effectiveness. They also have a structure that shows evidence of some deliberate planning. The writer's control of English usage ranges from fairly reliable at 4 to confident and accomplished at 6.

6 Papers scored as a 6 tend to offer sophisticated ideas within an organizational framework that is clear and appropriate for the topic. The supporting statements are particularly effective because of their substance, specificity, or illustrative quality. The writing is vivid and precise though it may contain an occasional flaw.

5 Papers scored as a 5 are clearly organized with effective support for each of the writer's major points. The writing offers substantive ideas though the paper may lack the flair or grace of a 6 paper. The surface features are consistently under control despite an occasional lapse in usage.

4 Papers scored as a 4 show evidence of the writer's organizational plan. Support, though sufficient, tends to be less extensive or convincing than that found in papers scored as a 5 or 6. The writer generally observes the conventions of accepted English usage. Some errors are usually present, but they are not severe enough to interfere significantly with the writer's main purpose.

Lower-half papers either fail to convey a purpose sufficiently or lack one entirely. Consequently, their structure ranges from rudimentary at 3, to random at 2, to absent at 1. Control of the conventions of English usage tends to follow this same gradient.

3 Papers scored as a 3 usually show some evidence of planning or development. However, the organization is often limited to a simple listing or haphazard recitation of ideas about the topic, leaving an impression of insufficiency. The 3 papers often demonstrate repeated weaknesses in accepted English usage and are generally ineffective in accomplishing the writer's purpose.

2 Papers scored as a 2 are characterized by a marked lack of development or inadequate support for ideas. The level of thought apparent in the writing is frequently unsophisticated or superficial, often marked by a listing of unsupported generalizations. Instead of suggesting a clear purpose, these papers often present conflicting purposes. Errors in accepted English usage may seriously interfere with the overall effectiveness of these papers.

1 Papers scored as a 1 leave the impression that the writer has not only not accomplished a purpose but has not made any purpose apparent. The dominant feature of these papers is the lack of control. The writer stumbles both in conveying a clear plan for the paper and in expressing ideas according to the conventions of accepted English usage.

0 The zero score is reserved for papers which are blank, illegible, or written on a topic other than the one assigned.

Source: *The 1988 Tests of General Educational Development: A Preview*, American Council on Education, 1985. Used with permission.

HOW TO SCORE YOUR ESSAY

To score your essay, compare it with the following model essays. These model essays received scores of 3 and 5, respectively.

Compare your essay with the 3 model essay. If it is as good as the 3 model essay, then assign your essay a score of 3. If it is not as good as the 3 model essay, then refer back to the GED Essay Scoring Guide and use the descriptions of the 1 and 2 model essays to evaluate your essay. It should be easy to assign a score to your essay if you compare your essay with these model essays and their character trait analyses.

If your essay is better than the 3 model essay, compare it to the model essay that received a 5. If it is better than the 3 but not as good as the 5, then score your essay a 4. If your essay is better than the 5 model essay, then score your essay a 6.

In addition, look at the notes and character trait analyses that accompany the model essays. These comments explain the strengths and weaknesses of these essays.

Model Essay—Holistic Score 3

Point of view is undefined. The writer seems to prefer radio to television but point of view on either is vague. Specific examples of a point of view are needed.

Haphazard listing of vague ideas and generalized examples about the topic.

Point of view not clearly stated.

I enjoy listening to radio, especially when I'm driving my car. You can't watch television when you are driving. Radio is good for listening to music, unless you have a tape deck in your car. You can also get music on television but not as much as on radio.

Radio is better for news than television. I listen regularly to an all-news station. If you listen for about 30 minutes, you can find out everything that's happening. If you do that about four times a day, it's like reading a whole newspaper from cover to cover.

Television has pictures, and that's something radio can't give. The pictures make television news more interesting, but they don't cover as much as all-news radio. On a television news show, there are so many commercials that they don't have time to tell you about all the things that have been happening. On all-news radio, they have 24 hours a day to do it.

Besides, the television stations and networks are prejudiced. They don't report news against big business, they're more interested in big cities than all the small towns all over the USA, where most of the people live.

Character Trait Analysis

1 The writer's point of view is not clearly stated in the opening paragraph or elsewhere in the essay.

2 The second and third paragraphs discuss the topic but do not include any specific examples that would indicate the writer's point of view.

3 The third paragraph incorrectly implies that radio news is not supported by commercial advertising.

4 The final paragraph does not summarize the writer's point of view. In fact, we still do not know exactly what the writer's point of view is on this topic.

5 The essay contains many sentence fragments and run-on sentences. There are other problems with accepted English usage that interfere with the essay's effectiveness.

Model Essay—Holistic Score 5

Clear statement of the point of view.

I enjoy both radio and television. Although television and radio entertainment can be compared, it is not a good idea to call one better than the other. They are simply different and each one can be good in a way that the other cannot.

These two paragraphs contrast the strong and weak points of radio and television as entertainment media.

Television brings pictures into our living rooms—pictures of actors, dancers, chase scenes, and pie-in-the-face comedy. I enjoy the immediacy of this kind of entertainment. Even movies require that we go out to a theater or to a video store for our entertainment.

Specific, personal examples are used to illustrate the writer's point of view.

Radio cannot bring pictures into our home as television does. On the other hand, radio allows more "mental participation" on the part of the audience. A listener can imagine his or her favorite singer in close-up. We can "see" a comedy routine any way we like. I like listening to a radio drama and creating the setting in my own mind. These are things that are impossible to do with television, which lays out even the tiniest details right before our eyes.

Restatement of point of view.

It isn't necessary to call one medium better than the other. It's enough to say that both television and radio offer unique types of entertainment.

Character Trait Analysis

1   The clear statement of the writer's point of view in the first paragraph results in a tightly organized essay.

2   This essay is more interesting to read than the 3 essay because of this writer's command of the language and larger vocabulary.

3   The point of view is clear and consistent throughout the essay.

4   The essay flows smoothly and has few problems with usage. The examples are good but they do not paint the vivid picture that the examples in a 6 essay would produce.

5   The final paragraph summarizes the points made in the second and third paragraphs and restates the point made at the beginning.